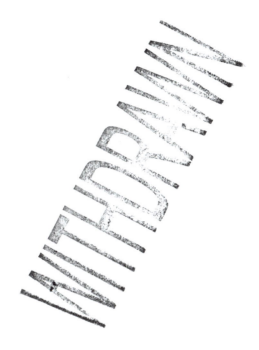

Supporting Readers in Secondary Schools

Supporting Readers in Secondary Schools

Wendy Jolliffe, David Waugh and Sue Beverton with Jayne Stead

Los Angeles | London | New Delhi
Singapore | Washington DC

Learning Matters
An imprint of SAGE Publications Ltd
1 Oliver's Yard
55 City Road
London EC1Y 1SP

SAGE Publications Inc.
2455 Teller Road
Thousand Oaks, California 91320

SAGE Publications India Pvt Ltd
B 1/I 1 Mohan Cooperative Industrial Area
Mathura Road
New Delhi 110 044

SAGE Publications Asia-Pacific Pte Ltd
3 Church Street
#10-04 Samsung Hub
Singapore 049483

Editor: Amy Thornton
Development Editor: Jennifer Clark
Production Controller: Chris Marke
Project Management: Deer Park Productions, Tavistock, Devon, England
Marketing Manager: Catherine Slinn
Cover design: Wendy Scott
Typeset by: C&M Digitals (P) Ltd, Chennai, India
Printed in Great Britain by
CPI Group (UK) Ltd, Croydon, CR0 4YY

© Wendy Jolliffe, David Waugh and Sue Beverton with Jayne Stead 2014

First published by Learning Matters SAGE 2014

Library of Congress Control Number: 2014932987

British Library Cataloguing in Publication data

A catalogue record for this book is available from the British Library

ISBN 978-1-4462-8062-1
ISBN 978-1-4462-8063-8 (pbk)

Contents

Acknowledgements

We would like to thank Aoife Kennedy of Durham University for providing extracts from her research on accents and phonics teaching, and Amy Roberts, formerly of Durham University and now teaching in the south of England, who provided extracts from her research on texting and spelling.

We are very grateful to all the teachers who shared their many exciting and interesting case studies with us. Thank you to the leadership team at Arnold Hill Academy for their generous gift of time to enable Jayne Stead to be able to contribute to the book. Thanks also go to the Learning and Coaching team at Arnold Hill – especially Clare Pedlar and the DT team whose primary liaison practice is exemplary. We are grateful to Arnold Hill Academy's feeder schools for being guinea pigs for new ideas and to all the schools who contributed ideas for case studies.

Finally, we are grateful to Rob Waugh, mathematics teacher at Sirius Academy, Hull, for sharing his ideas and acting as a sounding board for ours.

About the authors

Wendy Jolliffe

Wendy Jolliffe is Head of Scarborough School of Education for the University of Hull and has strategic responsibility for teacher education for primary, secondary and post compulsory education. She worked previously as a Regional Adviser for ITT for the National Strategies and advised ITT providers on effective provision for literacy. Wendy is a former deputy head teacher in a primary school in Hull and she has published extensively on teaching English and implementing Cooperative Learning.

David Waugh

David Waugh is Director of Primary PGCE at Durham University where he is also the subject leader for English. He has published extensively in Primary English. David is a former deputy head teacher, was Head of the Education Department at the University of Hull, and was Regional Adviser for ITT for the National Strategies from 2008 to 2010. As well as his educational writing, David also writes children's stories.

Sue Beverton

Sue Beverton is Director of Secondary PGCE at Durham University and is therefore involved in the initial training of secondary teachers across many subjects. She has worked extensively within initial teacher training for 13 years and before that worked for eight years leading an in-service MA for teachers in primary, secondary and tertiary education. As well as her teaching and training activities, Sue has conducted many research projects into various aspects of teaching and learning.

Jayne Stead

Jayne Stead is Director of Drama and Performing Arts at Arnold Hill Academy in Nottinghamshire. She has taught English and performing arts across Key Stages 3, 4 and 5 in a wide variety of schools. Jayne has undertaken extensive outreach work in primary schools and has advised on creative arts programmes at both secondary and primary levels. In her current role, Jayne leads an extensive curriculum in drama, art and music and is involved in the learning and teaching of literacy across the school, including transition from primary to secondary.

1 What is the role of phonics in the teaching of reading?

Learning outcomes

By reading this chapter you will develop an understanding of:

- key theoretical models of how children learn to read;
- the role phonics plays in learning to read and spell;
- the benefits of learning phonics for reading and spelling;
- different approaches to teaching phonics.

2012 Teachers' Standards

2. Promote good progress and outcomes by pupils:

- demonstrate knowledge and understanding of how pupils learn and how this impacts on teaching.

3. Demonstrate good subject and curriculum knowledge:

- demonstrate a critical understanding of developments in the subject and curriculum areas, and promote the value of scholarship;
- demonstrate an understanding of and take responsibility for promoting high standards of literacy, articulacy and the correct use of Standard English, whatever the teacher's specialist subject;
- if teaching early reading, demonstrate a clear understanding of systematic synthetic phonics.

Introduction

Learning to read is a complex process and yet most adults do not recall the process by which they became a reader. This is largely because, once automaticity is reached, as with other skills, such as driving, much of this becomes an unconscious process with the end point in mind. In the case of driving, the end point is getting to a destination: in the case of reading, it is understanding what is read. Research into the teaching of reading continues, more recently aided by advances in neuroscience and neuro-imaging techniques, which are beginning to shed light onto the processes taking place in the brain (Hruby and Goswami, 2011). Debates over the best methods to teach reading also continue, and fierce arguments rage over the place of phonics as opposed to other methods. This chapter aims to illuminate that debate through a review of the research evidence, but also to provide a balanced approach to enable teachers to be able to support readers. Nothing makes more of a difference to the progress students make in school than the ability to read and understand text, and therefore supporting readers who are experiencing difficulties is the task of every teacher whatever their subject or area of responsibility.

This chapter will support an overall understanding of the role phonics plays in teaching reading, and its benefits in reading as well as spelling. It will also provide an overview of the different types of phonics and what place these play in a balanced teaching programme.

Theoretical perspectives/subject knowledge
Learning to read

Learning to read involves two key aspects: first, the ability to decode the letters on the page, so that the letters can be mapped onto the sounds of our language (or phonemes) and then be pronounced, either aloud or silently, to make words. The second key process is to map these words to our lexicon, or mental store of known words, and in turn to combine these into units of meaning: phrases or sentences. It is vital to understand that these are integrated processes, and children learning to read require support with both elements. In essence: decoding is supported through learning phonics, which helps unlock the 'alphabetic code', in addition to acquiring a fast recall of high-frequency irregular words.

Achieving understanding of text is often termed 'language comprehension'. This is an umbrella term and not to be confused with narrow 'comprehension' activities. Language comprehension covers oral and written language and is multilayered. It spans understanding the words themselves, the ways the sentence is constructed, and the subjects of the text itself. Paris (2005) maintains that there are five essential skills in learning to read:

1. the alphabetic principle;

2. phonemic awareness;

3. oral reading fluency;

4. vocabulary;

5. comprehension.

He goes on to state that these skills need to be viewed differently as some are constrained; that is, once mastered (e.g. phonemic awareness or the alphabetic principle) they require little explicit teaching. Other skills, such as vocabulary and comprehension, require extended support.

In order to explain the processes involved in reading, researchers have constructed a number of models and an examination of the prominent ones follows.

The Simple View of Reading
The *Simple View of Reading* devised by Gough and Tunmer in 1986 focuses on two components: decoding and comprehension. *Decoding* means the ability to recognise

words out of context and to apply phonic rules to this recognition; thus it is termed 'word recognition'. *Comprehension* means *linguistic comprehension,* which is defined by Gough and Tunmer (1986) as the process by which words, sentences and discourse are interpreted. They also state that the two interrelated processes are both necessary for reading. This view has been developed since first proposed in 1986 and is represented in the Rose Review (DfES, 2006: 77) as shown in Figure 1.1 below.

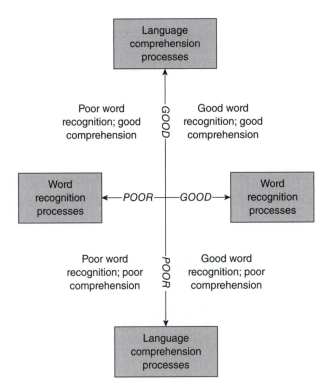

Figure 1.1   The Simple View of Reading

Source: DfES (2006) *Independent review of the teaching of early reading* (Final Report by Jim Rose). Ref: 0201/2006DOC-EN. Nottingham: DfES Publications, p 40.

The model is based on two axes and four quadrants, and children's strengths or weaknesses can be identified and categorised into the quadrants, enabling teaching to focus on specific aspects. As shown in Figure 1.2, it can support the diagnosis of reading difficulties.

The model asserts the importance of both word recognition and comprehension, and Gough and Tunmer (1986) propose that reading comprehension is the product of decoding and listening comprehension. Critics of the Simple View of Reading object principally to the oversimplification of what is a complex area. Hoover and Gough (1990, 2000) further developed this model into the *Reading Acquisition Framework* (see Figure 1.3), which subdivided language and comprehension and decoding into their

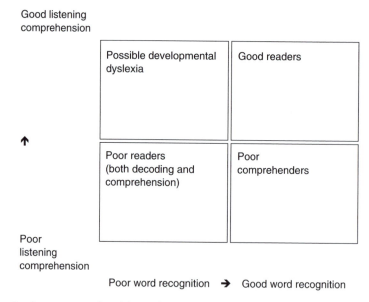

Good listening comprehension

| Possible developmental dyslexia | Good readers |
| Poor readers (both decoding and comprehension) | Poor comprehenders |

Poor listening comprehension

Poor word recognition   ➜   Good word recognition

Figure 1.2   Reader types predicted from the Simple View of Reading

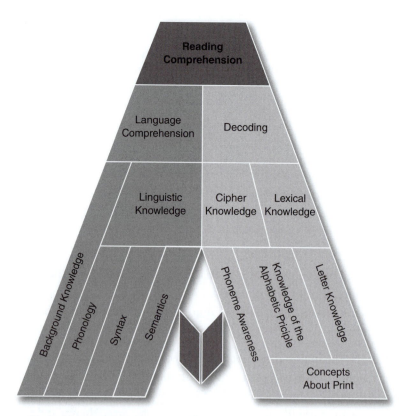

Figure 1.3   The Reading Acquisition Framework

Source: Wren, S. (2001) *The Cognitive Foundations of Learning to Read: a framework.* Austin,TX: Southwest Educational Development Laboratory, available at: www.sedl.org/cgibin/pdfexit.cgi?url=http://www.sedl.org/reading/framework/framework.pdf

4

constituent elements with two broad domains: *cipher knowledge* and *lexical knowledge*. Cipher knowledge concerns the systematic relationship between the letters and the sounds. Lexical knowledge consists of knowledge about words and, in particular, where the relationship between the units of spoken and written words does not follow a systematic pattern.

The word recognition system

Appendix 1 of the Rose Report (DfES, 2006), provides a diagrammatic version of the processes contained between seeing words and pronouncing them. This acknowledges the processes where the child either quickly recognises the word and then relates it to a store of word meanings or, if not, applies phonic rules in order to pronounce it and then relates the word to a lexicon of word meanings. This is shown in Figure 1.4.

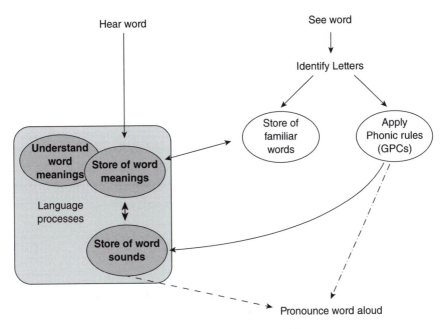

Figure 1.4 Diagrammatic representation of the word recognition system

Source: DFES (2006) *Independent Review of the Teaching of Early Reading* (Final Report by Jim Rose). Ref: 0201/2006DOC-EN. Nottingham: DfES Publications, p 86.

Strands of skilled reading

Scarborough (2009) provides a useful diagrammatic representation of the processes involved in skilled reading, as shown in Figure 1.5. Scarborough notes that:

> *Although most reading disabilities are associated with deficits in phonemic awareness, decoding and sight recognition of printed words, reading skill can also be seriously impeded by weaknesses in the comprehension strands, particularly beyond second grade when reading becomes more complex.*

(2009: 24)

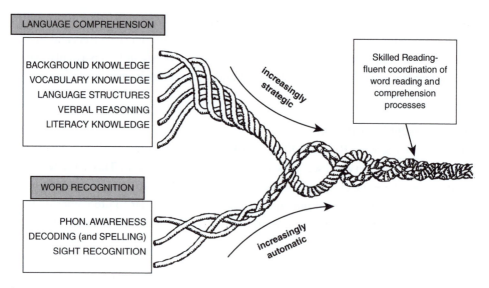

Figure 1.5   Strands of skilled reading

Source: Scarborough, H. (2009: 24) Connecting early language and literacy to later reading (dis)abilities: Evidence, theory and practice, in F. Fletcher-Campbell, J. Soler and G. Reid, *Approaching difficulties in literacy development: Assessment, pedagogy and programmes.* Los Angeles CA: Sage, pp 23–38.

Unlike the Simple View of Reading, therefore, this model proposes that weaknesses in reading comprehension may not be purely the product of weak decoding or listening comprehension. They could also be linked to vocabulary knowledge. For secondary school students, being faced with a growing range of words across subjects, this is a significant factor for students experiencing difficulties.

Activity 1.1   Applying theoretical models to practice

The models above are complex and abstract. Read the discussion below between two secondary school trainee teachers who have been studying the teaching of reading and the different models and applying them to their practice to see if this helps in understanding them.

Stan: *I've been reading about the models that explain how we learn to read and thinking about students in classes I teach to apply this. Take Jamie in Year 7, who is a very lively student with plenty to say and a very good vocabulary, but when he is faced with text he obviously struggles. I was surprised the other day that he found the words 'tornado' and 'hurricane' difficult. How do these models help explain his problems?*

Marie: *He obviously doesn't have very good decoding skills with unfamiliar words. Did he know what the words mean once you told him?*

Stan: *Yes — he went on to tell me all about 'twisters' and freak weather as he had seen a documentary about it. Do you think his problems are around decoding then?*

Marie: *Yes, it sounds like it. If you look at the Simple View of Reading, he would be in the top left quadrant, but it would be important to get an assessment done of exactly what he needs support with. I think the model showing the strands of skilled reading is helpful as it shows the different elements in word recognition. I had a look at this model when I was thinking of Emily in Year 8. She seems fine at reading the words but when I ask her questions about it, she struggles. That puts her in the bottom right quadrant of the Simple View of Reading, but I wanted to know more about what might help her. Looking at the strands model, I began to see that it wasn't just a lack of vocabulary, but I think the language structures make it difficult for her. She was reading a sentence to do with wildlife conservation that said something like, 'Even today, humans are a tiger's most significant predator.' She knew what a predator is so it seems to be more about the unfamiliar, complex sentence construction. I am going to work on this with her and see if it helps her if I simplify sentences. Perhaps some paired reading with a more able reader would support her.*

Stan: *I like that idea of paired reading. Let me know how it goes as it might be something I can use.*

Consider if you can apply the models to students you teach and how this knowledge might help in providing appropriate support.

Activity 1.2   Models in practice

From the different models above, consider the strengths of each to support a teacher in effective intervention for struggling readers, using the prompts below.

Prompt	The Simple View of Reading	The word recognition system	Strands of skilled reading
Ease of diagnosing particular areas of difficulty			
The importance of developing a child's vocabulary			
The need for a store of high-frequency words			
Having background knowledge of the subject			

The place of phonics

The central question in the teaching of reading, and in particular in relation to word recognition, is the role of phonics. The most important question for teachers is to understand when to use phonics and how, and to base this on a clear understanding of what phonics contributes to learning to learn.

What is meant by phonics teaching?

This is an umbrella term that includes the development of phonemic awareness (ability to hear, discriminate and manipulate phonemes), and the ability to map the graphemes (letters or groups of letters) to phonemes (the smallest units of sound in a word). A further and important aspect is the ability to blend the phonemes to make words, or the reverse – the ability to segment words into their constituent phonemes.

How phonics helps decoding

As discussion of the models of the reading process above showed, one key element in effective reading is the ability to decode unfamiliar words. Phonics provides the key to unlocking the alphabetic code. More detail of the English alphabetic code is contained in the next chapter. Understanding this is crucial and being able to map the grapheme/phoneme correspondences, or letters to sounds, is a skill that supports reading and spelling.

Decoding the marks on the page (or letters and their combinations – graphemes) can be achieved in two ways. First, by visual whole-word recognition – previously called 'look and say' and taught using flash cards. While some children with good visual memories learn well this way, for others, and particularly those with a disability such as dyslexia, this is problematic. Even for those with good visual memory, there are times when they will need phonics to decode unfamiliar words, just as adults do.

Activity 1.3

Consider how you read the following words:

necrocytosis

lithiasis

erythrocyte

You probably broke the words into syllables and then used your phonic knowledge of mapping the letters to sounds to attempt to pronounce them. As efficient readers, you will use your phonic knowledge less than beginning readers, but you still make use of this skill.

When to teach phonics

As the example in Activity 1.3 showed, phonics is a useful strategy for decoding. In order to become proficient, it is important to learn how to map graphemes to phonemes (letters to sounds) early. Taught effectively in interactive and multisensory ways, phonics can be learned by young children as long as it is applied in reading and writing and alongside a broad and rich literacy diet. For older children who are struggling readers, it is important to diagnose exactly what gaps they have in their phonic knowledge and to provide intensive support for them to catch up. Chapter 6 will examine this in more detail. One of the key factors is to ensure that materials and methods are age-appropriate, and many of the case studies in this book provide some very good examples of doing this.

Methods of teaching phonics

The following principles support the effective teaching of phonics.

- Start teaching phonics with young children in Foundation Stage and progress quickly so they learn the full alphabetic code between the ages of six to seven.

- Ensure regular over-learning of phonemes taught.

- Provide opportunities for application of learning in reading and writing in every lesson.

- Use a multisensory approach so that children learn from simultaneous visual, auditory and kinaesthetic activities which reinforce essential phonic knowledge and skills.

- Teach how phonemes can be blended, in order, from left to right, 'all through the word', for reading.

- Teach how to segment words into their constituent phonemes for spelling and that this is the reverse of blending phonemes to read words.

- Teach children to apply phonic knowledge and skills as their first approach to reading and spelling, even if a word is not completely phonically regular.

- Teach high-frequency words that do not conform completely to grapheme/phoneme correspondence rules.

- Use level-appropriate decodable texts, in the early stages of children acquiring phonics, to support their reading.

- Ensure ongoing assessment of progress and early intervention for children who are not making expected progress.

For struggling older readers, it is important to carry out a detailed assessment of the students' areas of difficulty as noted above. Once this has been done, there is a range of published intervention programmes to support students (e.g., *Read Write Inc.*

Fresh Start, www.ruthmiskintraining.com, or *Quick Fix for Phonics*, Jolliffe, 2012). It is important to make teaching and the application in reading and writing age-appropriate and relevant. This can have a considerable impact on levels of motivation and students' belief in their own ability or self-efficacy.

Phonics supports the key skill of decoding the marks on the page. It is only one part of the range of skills required to be an effective reader, but it can provide the tools for readers who are struggling to succeed, and an intensive programme has been shown to be very effective. As Chapter 4 shows, phonics is also an important strategy in supporting spelling and, while the English language is irregular, knowledge of the common patterns or *rimes* can be a key factor in becoming a good speller. There are estimated to be about 37 rimes that provide nearly 500 English words (Wylie and Durrell, 1970: 787–91). More discussion of this can be found on pages 56–7 in Chapter 4.

Activity 1.4   The role of phonics

Read the examples of the students' profiles below and decide whether phonics teaching is appropriate in both cases.

Student 1   *James is quite competent orally and appears to be better at reading than he really is. He shows some phonics skills and blends short words using phonics but is less secure with long vowel phonemes. For example, he knows that double 'o' makes the sound 'oo' in the word 'fool', but does not realise that the same sound is also made by 'ue' (blue), 'ew' (blew), 'oe' (shoe), 'ough' (through), 'wo' (two) and 'o' (to).*

Student 2   *Sara is a pupil with limited reading experiences and poor oral vocabulary. She has 'cracked the code' of reading, but the effort of decoding distracts her from the overall purpose of reading – making sense of the printed word. Unlike good readers who know when the text does not make sense and reread, she will often continue decoding even though she has lost the thread of what she is reading. She has largely sorted out the relationship between letters and sounds, but lacks the reading experience and vocabulary to comprehend simultaneously as she reads.*

Types of phonics teaching

The teaching of phonics includes a range of methods. There are two main types of phonics.

1. Systematic synthetic phonics is phonics taught in a systematic progression with the core aspect being the use of synthesis of sounds or blending in order to apply the skill to reading words, and the reversible skill of segmenting words into their

constituent sounds. This has been termed a 'part-to-whole' approach, because in this method children are taught to decode words by sounding out the letters and blending or synthesising them together.

2. Analytic phonics is where phonics is taught through analogy with words, i.e. if a child can read 'can', he/she can also read 'pan', 'fan', 'man', etc. by substituting different initial consonants or consonant blends. This has been termed a 'whole-to-part' approach in contrast to synthetic phonics, and it takes advantage of children's early awareness of onsets (the first part of the word before the vowel) and rimes (the rest of the word including the vowel, e.g. 'at' in 'hat'). In this approach children are taught to recognise patterns in words. Thus, they start with whole words and then break the words down into parts.

A third type of phonics teaching is referred to as contextual phonics (where phonics instruction is integrated with reading comprehension training using meaningful experiences with engaging texts). However, it is possible to ensure any phonics teaching is done alongside developing language comprehension and therefore to promote both main aspects of the Simple View of Reading together.

The approach recommended by the Government in England is systematic synthetic phonics and this is reinforced by three large international reports: the National Reading Panel report in the US in 2000, the Australian Government Review in 2005 and the Rose Report in the UK in 2006. The advantages cited for this approach are as follows.

- It ensures a systematic progression where all the major letter–sound correspondences (grapheme–phoneme correspondences or GPCs) are taught fast and early, which enables children to apply them in reading and writing.

- It provides opportunities for all children to make progress without a need to rely on skills such as visual memory.

- It can and should be embedded within a broad and language-rich curriculum.

- It can be taught in lively interactive ways using multisensory teaching methods.

- A range of research studies shows that systematic phonics instruction produces superior results.

- As English is more complex than many languages, a systematic approach to teaching the alphabetic code is beneficial, as stated in the Rose Review: *It cannot be left to chance, or for children to ferret out, on their own, how the alphabetic code works* (DfES, 2006: 19).

Criticisms of the systematic synthetic phonics approach centre around a reliance on phonics to the possible exclusion of meaningful engagement with text in order to foster a love of reading. Wyse and Goswami (2008: 691), in particular, have stated that there is no 'reliable empirical evidence' to show that synthetic phonics is the best approach for beginning readers. However, there is evidence to show that: *for readers of alphabetic languages, a child's phonological awareness and letter knowledge at school entry are two of the best predictors of reading success* (Cain, 2010: 172). It is also important to note that for struggling older readers, there is considerable evidence that a deficit in phonological processing skills is the main cause of reading failure (Adams, 1990; Share, 1995; Stanovitch, 1991; National Reading Panel, NICHD, 2000). It is also clear that for those with phonological deficits these are likely to persist in adulthood (Ball, 1996; Greenberg *et al.*, 1997).

Research focus: government reports

Much of the focus on phonics in the UK has stemmed from a research study carried out in Clackmannanshire, Scotland. Rhona Johnston and Joyce Watson (2005) looked at 300 children in the first year of the Scottish primary school system. They compared three different teaching methods: synthetic phonics; analytic phonics; and an analytic phonics method that included systematic phonemic awareness teaching. At the end of the programme, those children who had been taught by synthetic phonics were found to be seven months ahead of the other two groups in reading.

The Clackmannanshire report was widely influential and led to the review undertaken by Sir Jim Rose into the teaching of reading. The final report for the Secretary of State for Education and Skills produced in March 2006 (DfES, 2006) drew on research findings, consultation with practitioners, teachers, trainers, resource and policy makers and visits to schools and training events. The review made the following recommendations of best practice in the teaching of early reading and phonics:

- High-quality, systematic phonic work as defined by the review should be taught. The knowledge, skills and understanding that constitute high-quality work should be taught as the prime approach in learning to decode (to read) and encode (to write/spell) print.

- Phonic work should be set within a broad and rich language curriculum that takes full account of developing the four interdependent strands of language: speaking, listening, reading and writing, and enlarging children's stock of words.

- For most children, high-quality, systematic phonic work should start by the age of five, taking full account of professional judgements of children's developing abilities and the need to embed this work within a broad and rich curriculum. This should be preceded by pre-reading activities that pave the way for such work to start.

- Phonic work for young children should be multisensory in order to capture their interest, sustain motivation, and reinforce learning in imaginative and exciting ways.

The recommendations of the Rose Review have since been widely adopted, first by the Labour Government and then strengthened under the Coalition Government since 2010. Measures to monitor the adoption have included a specific focus by Ofsted for the inspection of schools and teacher training providers; and in the Teacher Standards in 2012, a specific statement that to gain qualified teacher status trainees should:

→

if teaching early reading, demonstrate a clear understanding of systematic synthetic phonics.

(DfE, 2011: para 3)

In the United States, the National Reading Panel (NRP) report by the National Institute of Child Health and Human Development (NICHD, 2000: 2–89) provided a meta-analysis of research into the teaching of reading and concluded that:

systematic phonics instruction proved to be universally effective, it should be implemented as part of literacy programs to teach beginning reading, as well as to prevent and remediate reading difficulties.

The NRP findings from a meta-analysis of evidence-based research indicated that, for beginning reading, direct, systematic instruction in phonics makes significantly greater contributions to children's development in reading, writing, spelling and comprehension than alternative approaches involving unsystematic or no phonics instruction. The NRP also emphasised that *systematic phonics instruction should be integrated with other reading instruction to create a balanced reading program* (pp. 2–136) and that it should not dominate the teaching of reading.

In Australia, a review of research into the teaching of reading (Australian Government, Department of Education, Science and Training, 2005: 25) also concluded:

the incontrovertible finding from the extensive body of local and international evidence-based reading research is that for children during the early years of schooling, they must first master the alphabetic code via systematic, explicit, and intensive instruction in: phonemic awareness, phonics, reading fluency, vocabulary, and reading comprehension strategies. Because these are foundational and essential skills for the development of competence in reading, writing and spelling, they must be taught early, explicitly, and taught well.

Based on such a range of studies, Snowling and Hulme (2005: 518) conclude that:

In our view, then, the findings from a wide array of sources – studies of reading development, studies of specific instructional practices, studies of teachers and schools found to be effective – converge on the conclusion that attention to small units in early reading instruction is helpful for all children, harmful for none, and crucial for some. This finding is richly supported in studies done both in the US (NRP, 2000) and the UK (Hatcher, Hulme, and Snowling, 2004).

Reading intervention projects

Torgesen *et al.* (2001: 35) stated that *our current understanding of the most common form of reading disability suggests that for children with reading disabilities to achieve adequate reading skills, they must receive more intensive, explicit, and systematic instruction in word-level skills than is typically provided in schools.* They maintain that the 'core characteristic' of such children is *a primary limitation in skilled use of the alphabetic principle.* A comparative study of two intervention programmes for children aged ten

→

who demonstrated reading disability, compared phonics programmes. The intervention programmes took under nine weeks and contained over 60 hours of tuition followed by a further follow-up of support for another eight weeks. One contained more emphasis on phonemic awareness and more extensive de-contextualised phonemic decoding skills. The other programme was described as embedded phonics and focused more on reading and writing connected text. Torgesen *et al.* found that the intensive phonemic treatment showed greater improvement initially. However, in a two-year follow-up assessment, both types of intervention proved to be effective in maintaining the improvement and both groups of children demonstrated substantial progress over the period, with about half of the children attaining average-level reading skills. This provides evidence that extensive intervention, which includes explicit phonics teaching for children who show severe reading difficulties, can be effective. The study also noted that the use of skilled teachers of reading is a further contributory factor as is shown in the case study below.

Case study: The school phonics expert

A school in the East Midlands has an excellent approach to literacy across the curriculum. They are further forward than most in recognising that *all teachers are teachers of literacy* (Bullock, 1975), with relevant and interesting word banks displayed in classrooms, specific glossaries in every subject, regular professional development training for staff and strategies for differentiation all well established and successful. However, this does not often include phonics. Clearly the teachers know what phonics is and appreciate its importance but have no real understanding of recent legislation and – beyond their skilled English department – do not regularly use phonics as one of their literacy strategies. It seems that staff see it very much as a priority for primary schools. Realising that if *they* felt like that then no doubt the *students* would too, they decided to have this as a literacy focus for their next phase of development.

A member of the school's learning/teaching coaching team was chosen to be the school's 'phonics expert'. In an effort to promote literacy across all subjects they did not go for the obvious choice of David in the English department but chose Claire – a technology teacher who already had contact with primary schools through her regular visits one day a week as the school's primary liaison link. Quickly realising that children as young as five and above know what a *phoneme,* a *grapheme* and *digraphs* are as well as being aware of *blending* and *segmenting,* she became convinced that secondary colleagues needed to know too if they were ever to build them into their strategies for their own classrooms.

Claire carried out the following methods of support.

- She established meetings to secure her own understanding with several primary literacy co-ordinators.

- She observed several classes where phonics was being taught – especially in Year 6 – to have a better idea of transition levels.

- She planned and taught several exercises and lessons with the primary co-ordinators and taught them in the primary school when delivering her usual lessons and workshops; i.e. she embedded them within her subject rather than delivered discrete phonics lessons.

- She planned and taught similar exercises and lessons in the secondary school – again embedding them within the lesson.

- She changed a display in her classroom built around her subject's key terminology, serving as a reminder to incoming Year 7s that phonics was still important – comforting and instantly recognisable for them.

- She met her coaching team and the curriculum leaders in the school for training where videoed lessons were shown, displays discussed and links established.

- She developed phonic starter games that were part of the school's 'Shout Out' strategy of sharing good practice and these were then used by all teachers.

- She led strategy sessions in the weekly CPD literacy sections and time was given for all staff to look at their schemes of work and literacy policies.

It has been a success. Phonics is becoming an established part of literacy learning in all subject areas. Starters and games take note of them, terminology is displayed in spelling segments and emphasises blending of words on the walls in classrooms. Now all teachers are beginning to realise that it is their responsibility to continue the good work begun in the primary classrooms. Students continue to grow up with phonic understanding as a tool to support their literacy.

National Curriculum links

The 2014 National Curriculum makes clear the expectations for decoding using phonics and states in Year 1 that:

Pupils should be taught to apply phonic knowledge and skills as the route to decode words.

By Key Stage 3, the expectation is that:

Pupils should be taught to develop an appreciation and love of reading, and read increasingly challenging material independently.

In this chapter you have reviewed theoretical models of learning to read which have shown that phonics plays a part in the decoding of text and that struggling readers often (but not always) show deficiencies in phonemic knowledge. You have also explored the different types of phonics teaching and principles of good phonics teaching.

Learning outcomes review

You should now know:

- key theoretical models of how children learn to read;
- the role phonics plays in learning to read and spell;
- the benefits of learning phonics for reading and spelling;
- different approaches to teaching phonics.

Self-assessment questions

1. What are the two key areas involved in learning to read?
2. What role does phonics play in both reading and spelling?
3. What is the main difference between synthetic and analytic phonics?
4. What are some of the principles of effective phonics teaching?

Activities: answers and discussion

Activity 1.2   Models in practice

Prompt	The Simple View of Reading	The word recognition system	Strands of skilled reading
Ease of diagnosing particular areas of difficulty	Can help diagnose difficulties within language comprehension or word recognition		
The importance of developing a child's vocabulary			Vocabulary plays a key part in comprehension of text
Support for accessing unfamiliar words		Demonstrates that word recognition strategies are required such as phonics	
The need for a store of high-frequency words		Helps in fast recognition of high-frequency words	
Having background knowledge of the subject			Identifies it as a key component

Activity 1.4   The role of phonics

Student 1 has gaps is his phonics knowledge, particularly in long vowel phonemes, and would benefit from further teaching based on assessment of his difficulties.

Student 2 is relying too heavily on phonics for decoding and has developed good knowledge of phonics. She would benefit from support in reading fluency and vocabulary extension.

Further reading

For the research behind the Simple View of Reading see, particularly Appendix 1:
DfES (2006) *Independent review of the teaching of early reading* (final report by Jim Rose).
Ref: 0201/2006DOC-EN. Nottingham: DfES Publications.

For an overview of the teaching of reading, see:
Waugh, D. and Jolliffe, W. (2012) *English 5–11*. London: Routledge (Chapter 7,
Teaching and learning reading).

For more on theoretical models of reading, see:
Grabe, W. and Stoller F. L. (2011) *Teaching and researching reading.* (2nd edn). Harlow: Pearson.

For an example of an intervention project, see:
Jolliffe, W. (2012) *Quick fix for phonics*. Witney: Scholastic.

References

Adams, M. (1990) *Beginning to read: Thinking and learning about print.* Cambridge, MA:
MIT Press.

Australian Government, Department of Education, Science and Training (2005)
Teaching reading: Literature review. A review of the evidence-based research literature
on approaches to the teaching of literacy, particularly those that are effective in
assisting students with reading difficulties. National Inquiry into the teaching of
literacy.

Ball, E. W. (1996) Phonological awareness and learning disabilities: Using
research to inform our practice. *Advances in Learning and Behavioural Disabilities*,
10: 77–100.

Cain, K. (2010) *Reading development and difficulties.* Chichester: BPS Blackwell.

Coltheart, M., Rastle, K., Perry, C., Langdon, R. and Ziegler, J. (2001) DRC: A dual
route cascaded model of visual word recognition and reading aloud. *Psychological
Review,* 108: 204–56.

DES (1975) *A Language for life: The Bullock Report.* London: HMSO.

DfE(2011) *Teachers' standards in England.* London: Department for Education.

DfES (2006) *Independent review of the teaching of early reading* (final report by Jim Rose).
Ref: 0201/2006DOC-EN. Nottingham: DfES Publications.

Gough, P. B. and Tunmer, W. E. (1986) Decoding, reading and reading disability.
Remedial and Special Education, 7, 6–10.

Greenberg, D., Ehri, L. C. and Perin, D. (1997) Are word-reading processes the same
or different in adult literacy students and third–fifth graders matched for reading level?
Journal of Educational Psychology, 89: 262–75.

Hoover, W. A. and Gough, P. B. (1990) The simple view of reading. *Reading and
Writing: An Interdisciplinary Journal*, 2: 127–60.

Hoover, W. A. and Gough, P. B. (2000) The reading acquisition framework, in S. Wren (ed.) *The Cognitive Foundations of Learning to Read: A Framework* (www.sedl.org/reading/framework) (accessed 2 January 2014).

Hruby, G. and Goswami, U. (2011) Neuroscience and reading: A review for education researchers. *Reading Research Quarterly*, 46 (2): 156–72.

Johnston, R. and Watson, J. (2005) *The effects of synthetic phonics teaching on reading and spelling attainment: A seven year longitudinal study,* published by the Scottish Executive, February 2005.

National Institute of Child Health and Human Development. (2000) *Report of the National Reading Panel. Teaching children to read: An evidence-based assessment of the scientific research literature on reading and its implications for reading instruction* (NIH Publication No. 00-4769). Washington, DC: US Government Printing Office.

Paris, S. G. (2005) Reinterpreting the development of reading skills. *Reading Research Quarterly,* 40 (2): 194–202.

Plaut, D. C., McClelland, J. L., Seidenberg, M. S. and Patterson, K. (1996) Understanding normal and impaired word reading: Computational principles in quasi-regular domains. *Psychological Review,* 103: 56–115.

Scarborough, H. S. (2009) Connecting early language and literacy to later reading (dis) abilities: Evidence, theory and practice, in Fletcher-Campbell, F., Soler, J. and Reid, G. *Approaching difficulties in literacy development: Assessment, pedagogy and programmes.* Los Angeles, CA: Sage, pp 23–38.

Seidenberg, M. S. (2005) Connectionist models of word reading. *Current Directions in Psychological Science,* 14: 238–42.

Share, D. L. (1995) Phonological recoding and orthographic learning: Sine qua non of reading acquisition. *Cognition*, 55: 151–218.

Snowling, M. J. and Hulme, C. (2005) *The science of reading: A handbook*. Malden, MA: Blackwell Publishing.

Stanovitch, K. E. (1991) Discrepancy definitions of reading disability: Has intelligence led us astray? *Reading Research Quarterly*, 26: 7–29

Torgesen, J. K., Alexander, A. W., Wagner, R. K., Rashotte, C. A., Voeller, K. S. and Conway, T. (2001) Intensive remedial instruction for children with severe reading disabilities: Immediate and long-term outcomes from two instructional approaches. *Journal of Learning Disabilities,* 34 (1): 33–58.

Wylie, R. E. and Durrell, D. D. (1970) Teaching vowels through phonograms. *Elementary English*, 47: 787–91.

Wyse, D. and Goswami, U. (2008) Synthetic phonics and the teaching of reading. *British Educational Research Journal,* 34 (6): 691–710.

2 Understanding the alphabetic code

Learning outcomes

By reading this chapter you will develop an understanding of:

- the English alphabetical system in which approximately 44 sounds are represented by 26 letters;
- the difference between the basic and the complex alphabetic code;
- the key terminology;
- how to support pupils in using and applying the alphabetic code for reading and spelling.

2012 Teachers' Standards

2. Promote good progress and outcomes by pupils:

- demonstrate knowledge and understanding of how pupils learn and how this impacts on teaching.

3. Demonstrate good subject and curriculum knowledge:

- demonstrate a critical understanding of developments in the subject and curriculum areas, and promote the value of scholarship;
- demonstrate an understanding of and take responsibility for promoting high standards of literacy, articulacy and the correct use of Standard English, whatever the teacher's specialist subject;
- if teaching early reading, demonstrate a clear understanding of systematic synthetic phonics.

Introduction

The alphabetic code, or principle, is based on the concept that letters, or combinations of letters, are used to represent the speech sounds of our language. In contrast, in some other languages such as Chinese or Japanese, the symbols used represent morphemes (or units of meaning) rather than the sounds of the language. In English, we use the letters of the alphabet often alone (the basic code), often in twos and in groups of three and four (advanced code), to represent the sounds in our language. There is not a direct correspondence between the 26 letters of the alphabet and the 44 phonemes in English, unlike other European languages where the correspondence is more transparent. Finnish, for example, is nearly completely regular, as are Italian, Swedish, Norwegian and German. It is this complexity in English that has led to a lack of use of phonics for teaching reading. It also demands a clear understanding by teachers of the *advanced* or *complex code* in order to teach it. To summarise, the English alphabetic code is underpinned by the following concepts.

- Sounds/phonemes are represented by letters/graphemes.

- A phoneme can be represented by one or more letters, for example the phoneme /igh/ can be written as 'i' (in tiger), 'i-e' (in time), or 'igh' (in light). A one-letter grapheme is called a graph; a two-letter grapheme a digraph; a three-letter grapheme a trigraph; and occasionally a four-letter grapheme a quadgraph (as in 'eight' = /eigh/ /t/).

- The same phoneme can be represented (spelled) more than one way, as in /ae/ spelled as 'ay' in play, or 'a-e' as in 'make' or 'ai' as in 'trail' or 'a' as in 'baby'.

- The same grapheme (spelling) may represent more than one phoneme, as demonstrated by the letter 'c' which may make the sound /s/ in 'city', or /c/ in 'cat'.

(See Chapter 4 to see how this impacts upon spelling.)

Theoretical perspectives/subject knowledge

The English language has approximately 44 phonemes, although there are estimated to be about 176 common ways of spelling these using 26 letters, which accounts for the complexity. The 44 phonemes are divided into consonant and vowel phonemes as follows:

24 consonant phonemes	18 of these have a close match between the letter and the sound it represents in a word and are easiest to learn;
	Six further consonant phonemes are mostly digraphs: /sh/, /ch/, /ng/ /th/ (as in 'thin'), /th/ (as in 'then'), and /zh/ (as in 'television');
20 vowel phonemes	Five short vowels /a/ as in 'cat', /e/ as in 'peg', /i/ as in 'bit', /o/ as in 'dog' and /u/ as in 'hut';
	Five long vowels where the vowel 'says the letter name' (/ay/, /ee/, /igh/, /oa/ and /oo/);
	These long vowel phonemes can also be represented as 'split digraphs' (two letters split by a consonant, as in the /ay/ sound in 'make');
	Nine further more complex long vowel phonemes which have a range of spelling choices: /ar/ (car), /ur/ (burn), /or/ (corn), /oo/ (book), /ow/ (cow), /oi/ (coin), /air/ (hair), /ear/ (fear), /ure/ (sure);
	There is also one unstressed vowel, /ə/ the 'schwa' phoneme, pronounced as 'uh' is in 'collar'.

It is useful to break down the alphabetic code, particularly for teaching purposes, between the basic and the complex code as set out below.

The basic code

The basic code refers to the concept that a single letter makes a sound. Children need to begin by learning one spelling for about 40 of the approximately 44 phonemes in the English language. It is common for phonics programmes to start by teaching a few consonants and short vowel phonemes (e.g. /s/ /a/ /t/ /p/ /i/ /n/) and then move into blending these into consonant-vowel-consonant (CVC) words (e.g. 'sat', 'tin', 'pin', etc.).

Children need to then progress quickly to learn the more complex alphabetic code, in order to understand the alternative ways of representing the 44 phonemes. When phonics teaching focused on 'one letter makes one sound', as was common previously, it soon became obsolete, as children discovered with their own names, for example, Sophie, Chloe and Christopher, which do not comply with this basic code.

The complex code

The complex code involves the representation of a phoneme by one or sometimes more letters; it shows that the same phonemes can be spelled differently; and the same grapheme can represent different phonemes. There are several factors that add to the complexity here, as outlined below.

One phoneme – one or more letters

There are many examples of the same phoneme being represented by a combination of one or more than one letter, as shown with the consonant phonemes below.

Phonemes	Common spellings
/s/	sun, mouse, city, mess, science, mice
/t/	tap, better
/p/	paper, hippo
/n/	noise, knife, gnat
/d/	dog, puddle
/m/	man, hammer, comb
/g/	game, egg
/c/ /k/	cat, Chris, king, luck, queen
/r/	rabbit, wrong, berry
/b/	baby, cabbage
/f/	fish, photo, coffee
/l/	leg, spell
/sh/	ship, mission, chef
/z/	zebra, please, is, fizzy, sneeze
/w/	water, wheel, queen
/ch/	chip, watch
/j/	jug, judge, giant, barge
/v/	van, drive

The same phoneme – different spelling

This is another common factor in the English language, that the same phoneme can be represented in different ways, as in the example below.

Phoneme	Common spellings
/au/	sauce, horn, door, warn, claw, ball

The same grapheme – different phoneme

In addition, the same spelling, or grapheme, can represent different phonemes, as the example below shows:

Grapheme	Phoneme
ch	/ch/ in 'church', /sh/ in 'chef' or /k/ in 'school'

Terminology

One of the reasons why phonics seems so complex is the amount of terminology used that is unfamiliar. However, even young children are taught to use the correct terms, therefore it is important for teachers of older secondary students to fully understand these terms. Many of the terms have already been used in this chapter, so now see if you can match the definitions to the terms. The version below has the terms and definitions muddled. You will find the correct versions on page 31.

Activity 2.1   Understanding terminology

Term	Correct definition	Select a definition
Phoneme		1. One letter making one sound
Grapheme		2. Two letters which combine to make a new sound
Graph		3. The smallest single identifiable sound, e.g. the letters 'ch' representing one sound
Segmenting		4. Two letters, making one sound, e.g. a-e as in 'cake'
Digraph		5. A letter or combination of letters that represent a phoneme
Trigraph		6. To draw individual sounds together to pronounce a word, e.g. /c/l/a/p/, blended together reads 'clap'
Blending		7. Three letters which combine to make a new sound
Split digraph		8. Splitting up a word into its individual phonemes in order to spell it, i.e. the word 'pat' has three phonemes: /p/a/t/

The schwa phoneme

One of the difficulties of English is that the most frequent phoneme in the language, the 'schwa' phoneme /∂/, is the most common in our language and has the greatest variation. It causes two principal problems, first the sheer variety of ways of spelling it:

'er' in 'teacher', 'e' in 'wooden', 'u' in circus, 'ar' in 'collar', 'or' in 'doctor'.

The second problem is that in enunciating phonemes it is important to pronounce them without the 'schwa', an unstressed vowel or extra sound added to some phonemes. Ofsted (2011a: 20) has reiterated the importance of this:

correct articulation is vital in helping children to learn to blend sounds together. This means making sure that the sound produced (each individual phoneme) is as precise and accurate as possible and that no additional sounds are added. For instance, the sound /m/ that starts 'mother' or is embedded in 'impress' needs to sound /mmmm/ and not /muh/. The clearer the sound, the easier it is for a child to blend together (synthesise) the individual sounds to read a word because there are no unnecessary sounds getting in the way.

Research focus: Spelling and reading

Learning to spell and learning to read rely on the same underlying knowledge about the language, specifically the relationships between letters and sounds, and as Moats and Snow (2005) note, spelling instruction can be designed to help children better understand that key knowledge, resulting in better reading (Ehri, 2000). Snow *et al.* (2005: 86) comment on the real importance of spelling for reading as follows:

> *Spelling and reading build and rely on the same mental representation of a word. Knowing the spelling of a word makes the representation of it sturdy and accessible for fluent reading.*

In addition, Ehri and Snowling (2004) found that the ability to read words 'by sight' (i.e. automatically) rests on the ability to map letters and letter combinations to sounds. According to Hanna *et al.* (1966), half of all English words can be spelled accurately on the basis of sound–symbol correspondences alone.

Research for centuries has shown that spelling has a fundamental success rate in relation to reading. Webster (1783), in analysing the English alphabetic code, recognised this when he wrote a 'speller' and not a 'reader' and put the emphasis on the links between successful spelling and reading. Maria Montessori (1912) also advised teachers to teach spelling first and then for children to use this to read what they have written. In 1985, Frith proposed a six-step model of learning to read and spell, to draw out children's early ability to hear sounds in words. Huxford *et al.* (1991) showed a progression in which children's ability to spell phonemically regular words preceded their ability to read them. The reading programme *Breakthrough to Literacy* (first published in 1969, Mackay *et al.*) advocated a complex system of using language folders with individual words on cards for children to construct sentences. Larger versions of 'sentence holders' and word cards enabled the teacher to model the process. Of course, this system relied on 'look and say' or whole-word recognition rather than phonics, but nevertheless, the principle of the interrelationship between writing and reading was present. This illustrates the importance of creating texts for children aligned to their phonic knowledge. Such texts can also be linked to a child's experiences and cultural background and are therefore more meaningful. This is an important consideration in creating age-appropriate texts for secondary-age students.

Expectations for secondary schools

Having a clear understanding of the alphabetic code is the basis of teaching phonics to support reading and spelling. Ofsted, in its report *Removing Barriers to Literacy* (2011b), noted that schools should:

- *raise the expectations of staff for pupils from low-attaining groups, especially in Year 7, and use all available assessment information to ascertain their literacy needs and to set them challenging targets; this is particularly important to establish suitable expectations for GCSE English language.*

(Ofsted, 2011b: 8)

In addition, the report noted that providers should:

- *ensure that learners without a grasp of phonics receive the necessary teaching.*

(Ofsted, 2011b: 9)

The following case study of good practice is cited (Ofsted, 2011: 29–30).

> *The students, taught in groups of seven, were given guidance based on familiar spelling rules that were relevant to their work in other subjects.*
>
> *As additional support for students whose reading problems were a barrier to their learning across the curriculum, the school considered ways of tackling gaps in their reading. For students in Years 7 and 8, the school decided to use a commercial scheme with all its withdrawal groups. The school chose this approach because it felt it would cover a number of areas where students' skills were weak: namely, phonic knowledge, reading comprehension, reading fluency and handwriting. Over five months, the average accelerated progress of a Year 7 pupil on the programme was:*
>
> - *7.4 months' gain in word reading;*
> - *9.1 months' gain in reading;*
> - *7.8 months' gain in spelling.*
>
> *The school invested time and resources in training teaching assistants to provide the programme effectively.*
>
> *Students on the programme sustained the gains they had made and the school's data showed how the initiative had narrowed the gap between these students and their peers in English and in other areas of the curriculum.*

For more information on effective assessment, which is essential in order to ensure students' needs are met, see Chapter 6.

Activity 2.2 Using the alphabetic code

Read aloud the sentence below, which is written using incorrect spelling choices for phonemes. Correct the spelling choices using your knowledge of the alphabetic code.

Tha cunn wrowss hie en tha scie.

You will find the correct version in the answers and discussion of the activities at the end of this chapter.

Reading sentences in old English demonstrates how the language has evolved, with different spelling choices becoming standard. For example, see the original 1597 version of Shakespeare's *Richard III*:

Now is the Winter of our Discontent,

Made glorious Summer by this Son of Yorke:

And all the clouds that lowr'd vpon our house

In the deepe bosome of the Ocean buried.

You will find more information about the history of English spelling in Chapter 4.

The international phonetic alphabet

In 1888, the International Phonetic Association published the International Phonetic Alphabet (IPA) which was designed to help regulate the sounds of spoken languages. It uses a range of symbols based on the Latin alphabet and, as many European languages have Latin roots, this makes sense. There are symbols for every sound in speech and 107 symbols in total to represent consonants and vowels. You will find more information on a number of websites, for example: www.antimoon.com/how/pronunc-soundsipa.htm.

The IPA can be a very useful tool when there is any confusion in identifying individual phonemes and many phonics schemes make use of it. The IPA can also be found in dictionaries, for example, the *Oxford English Dictionary*, so if you look up a word, you will see the phonetic pronunciation alongside it. The Department for Education refers to the IPA in relation to the Phonics Screening check introduced in 2012 for six-year-olds. It is also included as an appendix in the 2014 National Curriculum: https://www.gov.uk/government/collections/national-curriculum.

Phonemic awareness

One of the key aspects of successful learning in phonics is to have good phonemic awareness as, without it, children will struggle to make progress. It is first important to differentiate phonological awareness from phonemic awareness. Phonological awareness is a more general term to cover the different ways that oral language can be divided into smaller components and manipulated. McGuinness (2004: 368) describes phonological awareness as *the ability to hear and remember a variety of units of sound within words: syllables, syllable fragment (onset/rime), phoneme*. Phonemic awareness is more specific and relates to the ability to perceive and manipulate individual phonemes in spoken words and to remember the order of phonemes in words. An example would be to ask a child to tell you the phonemes in the word 'bat' – /b/ /a/ /t/ – and then, if you asked him to change the first letter of the word to make 'hat', the child would be able to say /h/ /a/ /t/. Share and Stanovich (1995) maintain that a lack of phonemic awareness is one of the most important causal factors separating non-impaired and impaired readers. It is therefore important to check that students are able to hear phonemes correctly when you are diagnosing difficulties.

Research focus: Phonemic awareness

Impaired readers, Dehaene (2009) found, suffered from poor phonemic awareness and faulty sound–symbol correspondence. In a large study in Milan, Paulesu *et al.* (2001) studied dyslexic brains, and found that when compared to non-impaired readers, they showed less activity in the anterior and posterior reading systems located on the left side of the brain, and more activity in right hemisphere sites. The right-side activity is thought to be attempting to compensate for the disrupted left-side systems (Shaywitz *et al.*, 2002). Research based on neuroscience using functional magnetic resonance imaging (fMRI) or positron emission tomography (PET) scanning is beginning to inform what occurs. However, as Hruby and Goswami (2011: 156) report, it is still early days and: *much more research on decoding processes in typically developing children is needed before profound implications for instruction can be expected.*

Activity 2.3   Different spelling choices for the same phoneme

How many different ways can you find to spell the /ee/ phoneme, as in 'green'?

How many different ways can you find to spell the /au/ phoneme, as in 'door'?

(There are at least nine ways for each.)

Supporting students in understanding the alphabetic code

It is important to assess students carefully before commencing any phonics tuition. One of the key aspects is to ensure that students do not become demotivated and perceive phonics teaching as 'babyish'. It therefore requires a different approach. There is a range of phonics intervention programmes that will support and some that are designed for older students. Some of the possible strategies that may support include the following.

1. Create raps to help students to recall phonemes. As phonemes are learned, sayings can be linked together to form a 'rap'. Said in a lively way at the start of each phonics lesson, this acts as revision or overlearning of the phonemes taught and can be a lively way of starting the lesson. Constant practice at saying this rap will support pupils in remembering the phonemes and their most common spelling choices/graphemes. Older students may like to create these for younger children also.

   When teaching the rap, it is important to follow these steps:

   (a) Say the phoneme twice, e.g. /ay/ay/;

   (b) Say the mnemonic, e.g. 'Play with hay';

   (c) Say the letter names, e.g. 'A Y'.

2. Help students who may struggle with multisyllabic words. Teaching could include the six syllable types in English and the rules for syllabification. For example, students can break down the word 'replace' by dividing it into an open syllable, 're' which keeps the long vowel sound and followed by the split digraph, or vowel-consonant-e syllable in 'place'. For a summary of the six syllable types, see: www.readingrockets.org/article/28653.

3. Encourage students to create their own texts for reading that are relevant to their particular interests.

4. Group students into co-operative learning groups and create 'literature circles' with students of mixed reading ability. This requires the following steps:

   (a) Select a range of books on themes such as trust, courage or fear. Gather books on the themes and let students choose a theme and then join a group around the theme.

   (b) Designate roles in groups, such as:

       • discussion leader: creates probing (Socratic) questions for discussion;

       • wordsmith: defines significant vocabulary;

- literary expert: illuminates the literary sections by reading aloud;

- character actor: role-plays characters, actions, motives, etc.;

- illustrator: captures key images from the reading;

- surveyor: graphs the plot line of the story.

(c) Students meet to discuss, share, and read aloud, using the assigned roles to keep the group moving along.

(d) Groups present key points of the book and share with other groups.

Research focus: Comparing alphabetic codes

The problem with the English language is that the code is opaque and there is not a direct correspondence between the 26 letters of the alphabet and the 40+ phonemes. In other languages, as noted above, this is not the case and the codes are more clearly reversible. Comparative studies of languages have provided clear evidence of the differences in the transparency of the alphabetic codes.

Venezky (1973) studied 240 Finnish children in grades 1 to 3 and found how easy it was to learn to read and write a transparent alphabet. Children begin reading in Finland at age seven. After one year of tuition, in a reading test of nonsense words denoting the complete Finnish orthography, the children scored 80 per cent and the same test administered to college students showed 90 per cent correct. This showed that it takes only about a year to gain proficiency in Finnish spelling.

Wimmer and Landerl (1997) compared Austrian and English children in a test of German and English words with similar complexity. The English children made twice the number of spelling errors as the Austrian children and, importantly, 90 per cent of the errors made by the Austrian children were phonemically accurate compared to only 32 per cent for the English children.

Geva and Siegel (2000) found a similar pattern in a study of 245 Canadian children who were learning to read and write both English and Hebrew together, with English as the first language. Hebrew is a transparent writing system that uses symbols for consonants and diacritic marks for vowels when texts are difficult, as for beginning readers. By the end of the first grade, the children scored 79 per cent correct on the Hebrew reading test but only 44 per cent correct on the English version of the test. Children did not achieve 80 per cent competency until the fifth grade.

Teaching phonics with older students requires innovative and engaging methods. For a good example of this, read the case study below of using interactive techniques incorporating phonics.

Case study: Soundscape

Ruth is an experienced English and Drama teacher in the secondary phase. She often uses drama conventions and techniques within her English work to give opportunities for kinaesthetic learning where difficult concepts or confidence can be an issue. During a phonics lesson where she wanted to build on the good practice in primary school, she created a 'sound orchestra' which she used in order to discriminate between phonemes in words. Gathering the students around in a circle, after a lively voice warm-up game, she asked the children to choose a sound for themselves from a careful selection projected onto the whiteboard (/m/ /d/ /s/ /t/ /f/ /c/). The only rule was that it must *not* be the same sound as that chosen by the person on either side of them. The teacher then asked them to close their eyes while she went around the outside of the circle and tapped each student on their back to prompt them to begin and end the sounds. Ruth and her class had great fun being a 'human xylophone' until they had built up their confidence in their enunciation. The teacher then stepped into the centre of the circle and 'conducted' the 'orchestra'. She pointed to start the sounds; raised her arms to indicate that the children should get louder; arms lowered meant still the same sound, but made in almost a whisper. Any volume in between had to be judged by the students, and as it was all one big happy team the students gained vocal confidence as well as almost forgetting that this was a lesson in phonics. The students then chose words, phrases and sentences that used their phoneme and the whole process began again – this time with students taking it in turns to be the 'conductor' themselves.

Activity 2.4   Checking your understanding

The alphabetic code quiz

In order to reinforce your understanding of the alphabetic code, now answer the following questions.

1. What is a phoneme?

2. What is a grapheme?

3. What is a digraph? Give an example.

4. What is a CVC word? Give an example.

→

5. How many phonemes are in the word 'strap'?

6. Which is the 'schwa' phoneme in the word 'teacher'?

7. What is the name of the grapheme that contains three letters?

8. Name several ways of spelling the /ai/ phoneme.

9. Segment 'reading' into phonemes.

10. Name a grapheme that can make different sounds or phonemes.

National Curriculum links

The 2014 National Curriculum makes clear the expectations for decoding using phonics and states in Year 1 that:

Pupils should be taught to apply phonic knowledge and skills as the route to decode words.

By Key Stage 3, the expectation is that:

Pupils should be taught to develop an appreciation and love of reading, and read increasingly challenging material independently.

In this chapter you have reviewed the key aspects of the English alphabetic code and its importance for reading and spelling. In spite of the complexities, it is possible to teach it even to young children. Students who struggle with reading often demonstrate difficulties in both understanding and applying the alphabetic code, particularly the complex code. It is therefore important to ensure that any gaps are identified and pupils are supported in order to gain the required literacy levels.

Learning outcomes review

You should now know

- the English alphabetical system in which approximately 44 sounds are represented by 26 letters;
- the difference between the basic and the complex alphabetic code;
- the key terminology;
- how to support pupils in using and applying the alphabetic code for reading and spelling.

Activities: answers and discussion

Activity 2.1   Understanding terminology

Term	Definition
Phoneme	The smallest single identifiable sound, e.g. the letters 'ch' representing one sound
Grapheme	A letter, or combination of letters, that represent a phoneme
Graph	One letter making one sound
Segmenting	Splitting up a word into its individual phonemes in order to spell it, i.e. the word 'pat' has three phonemes: /p/a/t/
Digraph	Two letters which combine to make a new sound
Trigraph	Three letters which combine to make a new sound
Blending	To draw individual sounds together to pronounce a word, e.g. /c/l/a/p/, blended together, reads 'clap'
Split digraph	Two letters, making one sound which are separated by a consonant, e.g. a-e as in 'cake'

Activity 2.2   Using the alphabetic code

Tha cunn wrowss hie en tha scie.

The sun rose high in the sky.

Activity 2.3   Different spelling choices for the same phoneme

The phoneme /ee/ (as in green) can be spelled in nine ways as follows:

'ea' (mean)

'e' (be)

'ie' (siege)

'ei' (deceive)

'e-e' (serene)

'ey' (key)

'y' (folly)

'I' (radio)

'i-e' (marine)

The phoneme /au/ (as in door) can be spelled in the following nine ways:

'au' (sauce)

'aw (claw)

'oar' (oar)

'or' (horn)

'a' (ball)

'ar' (warn)

'ure' (sure)

'oa' (broad)

'oor' (door)

Activity 2.4   Checking your understanding

Answers to the alphabetic code quiz

1. *What is a phoneme?*

   The smallest single identifiable sound in a word.

2. *What is a grapheme?*

   A letter, or combination of letters, that represents a phoneme.

3. *What is a digraph? Give an example.*

   Two letters which combine to make a new sound (e.g. 'ship')

4. *What is a CVC word? Give an example.*

   Consonant-vowel-consonant word, e.g. 'cat'.

5. *How many phonemes are in the word 'strap'?*

   Five – /s/t/r/a/p/

6. *Which is the 'schwa' phoneme in the word 'teacher'?*

   'er' – /t/ea/ch/**er**/

7. *What is the name of the grapheme that contains three letters?*

   trigraph

8. *Name several ways of spelling the /ai/ phoneme.*

   'ai', 'ay', 'a-e' and, less common, 'ei', 'eigh', 'ea', 'ey', 'aigh'.

9. *Segment 'reading' into phonemes.*

   /r/ea/d/i/ng/

10. *Name a grapheme that can make different sounds or phonemes.*

    's' as in 'sun' or 'laser'

Further reading

For more information on educational neuroscience and reading see:
Dehaene, S. (2009) *Reading in the brain: The science and evolution of a human invention.* New York: Viking.

For more information on methods of teaching phonics see:
Jolliffe, W., Waugh, D. with Carrs, A. (2012) *Teaching systematic synthetic phonics in primary schools.* London: Sage/Learning Matters (Chapters 4 and 5).

For more on the research background to understanding the alphabetic code see:
McGuinness, D. (2004) *Early reading instruction: What science really tells us about how to teach reading.* Cambridge, MA: MIT Press

References

Dehaene, S. (2009) *Reading in the brain: The science and evolution of a human invention.* New York: Viking.

Ehri, L. (2000) Learning to read and learning to spell: Two sides of a coin. *Topics in Language Disorders*, 20 (3): 19–49.

Ehri, L. and Snowling, M. J. (2004) Developmental variation in word recognition, in Stone, C. A., Silliman, E. R., Ehren, B. J. and Apel, K. (eds) *Handbook of language and literacy: Development and disorders*, pp. 433–60. New York: Guilford.

Frith, U. (1985) Beneath the surface of developmental dyslexia, in Patterson, J., Marshall, J. C. and Coltheart, M. (eds) *Surface dyslexia.* London: Erlbaum, pp. 301–30.

Geva, E. and Siegel, L. S. (2000) Orthographic and cognitive factors in the concurrent development of basic reading skills in two languages. *Reading and Writing: An Interdisciplinary Journal*, 12: 1–30.

Hanna, P. R., Hanna, J. S., Hodges, R. E. and Rudorf, E. H. Jr. (1966) *Phoneme–grapheme correspondences as cues to spelling improvement* (USDOE Publication No. 32008). Washington, DC: US Government Printing Office.

Hruby, G. and Goswami, U. (2011) Neuroscience and reading: A review for education researchers. *Reading Research Quarterly*, 46 (2):156–72.

Huxford, L., Terrell, C. and Bradley, L. (1991) *The relationship between the phonological strategies employed in reading and spelling.* London: Blackwell.

McGuinness, D. (2004) *Early reading instruction: What science really tells us about how to teach reading.* Cambridge, MA: MIT Press.

Mackay, D., Thompson, B. and Schaub, P. (1970) *Breakthrough to literacy: Teacher's manual.* London: Longman.

Moats, L. and Snow, C. (2005) How spelling supports reading. *American Educator* 1–13.

Montessori, M. (1912) *The Montessori method* (translated by Anne George). London: Heinemann.

Ofsted (2011a) *Getting them reading early* (ref: 110122). Manchester: Ofsted. Available at: www.ofsted.gov.uk/resources/getting-them-reading-early

Ofsted (2011b) *Removing barriers to literacy*. Manchester: Ofsted. Available at: www.ofsted.gov.uk/resources/removing-barriers-literacy

Paulesu, E., Demonet, J. F., Fazio, F., McCrory, E., Chanoine, V., Brunswick, N., Cappa, S. F., Cossu, G., Habib, M., Frith, C. D. and Frith, U. (2001) Dyslexia: Cultural diversity and biological unity. *Science*, 291 (5511): 2165–7.

Share, D. L. and Stanovich, K. E. (1995) Cognitive processes in early reading development: Accommodating individual differences into a model of acquisition. *Issues in Education: Contributions from Educational Psychology*, 1: 1–57.

Shaywitz, B. A., Shaywitz, S. E., Pugh, K. R., Mencl, W. E., Fulbright, R. K., Skudlarksi, P., Constable, R. T., Marchione, K. E., Fletcher, J. M., Lyon, G. R. and Gore, J. C. (2002) Disruption of posterior brain systems for reading in children with developmental dyslexia. *Biological Psychiatry*, 52 (2): 101–10. Retrieved from: www.ncbi.nlm.nih.gov/pubmed/12114001 (accessed 3 January 2014).

Snow, C. E., Griffin, P. and Burns, M. S. (eds) (2005) *Knowledge to support the teaching of reading: Preparing teachers for a changing world.* San Francisco: Jossey-Bass.

Venezky, R. L. (1973) Letter–sound generalizations of first, second, and third-grade Finnish children. *Journal of Educational Psychology,* 64: 288–92.

Webster, N. (1783) *A grammatical institute of the English language.* Part 1. Facsimile (1968). Menston, England: Scholar Press.

Wimmer, H. and Landerl, K. (1997) How learning to spell German differs from learning to spell English, in Perfetti, C. A., Rieben, L. and Fayol, M. (eds) *Learning to spell: Research, theory and practice across languages.* Mahway, NJ: Erlbaum, pp. 81–96.

3 Challenges

Learning outcomes

By reading this chapter you will develop:

- an understanding of the importance of correct enunciation of phonemes;
- an understanding of issues related to accent;
- a deeper understanding of phoneme and grapheme variation;
- strategies for supporting vocabulary development;
- an appreciation of some of the challenges which secondary teachers face when teaching reading and some strategies for addressing these.

2012 Teachers' Standards

2. Promote good progress and outcomes by pupils:

- demonstrate knowledge and understanding of how pupils learn and how this impacts on teaching.

3. Demonstrate good subject and curriculum knowledge:

- have a secure knowledge of the relevant subject(s) and curriculum areas, foster and maintain pupils' interest in the subject, and address misunderstandings;
- demonstrate an understanding of and take responsibility for promoting high standards of literacy, articulacy and the correct use of Standard English, whatever the teacher's specialist subject.

Key terminology

accent, dialect, schwa, enunciation, grapheme variation, phoneme variation

Introduction

This chapter will explore some of the key challenges which face teachers working in Key Stage 3 and Key Stage 4 to develop children's reading. You will see how the English alphabetic system presents challenges when we adopt a phonic approach to reading, and will explore ways of meeting this challenge, including the challenges presented by phonics programmes based upon an accent which may be quite different from those spoken by teachers and students. You will also look at some of the challenges presented because children have failed to acquire adequate reading skills to engage fully with the curriculum.

For children used to struggling with reading, the transfer to Key Stage 3 presents a number of challenges.

- Access to the curricula for a range of subjects will be difficult and they may quickly fall behind others, even where they understand and enjoy subjects' concepts.

- A lack of strategies for reading new words may prevent them from using worksheets, IT resources and other texts effectively.

- Whereas their primary teachers will have been trained to teach reading and should have been able to offer strategies and guidance across the curriculum, secondary teachers may be less sure about addressing reading difficulties.

- At Key Stage 3 children usually work with different teachers for different subjects, meaning teachers will not know individuals and their learning difficulties as well as primary teachers who typically teach most or all subjects to their classes.

Engaging students with the curriculum

A further problem can be finding texts which children who struggle with reading can read, and particularly finding texts which are appropriate for both the reading and the maturity level of the child. For children used to reading failure, a further diet of texts written for younger children may not engage their interest and will also be seen by the children as demeaning and may lead to low self-esteem. In the case study below, a teacher attempts to engage students' interest in text by involving popular culture which is familiar to them.

Case study: Rewriting lyrics

Tom is a music teacher in a large secondary school. His input to the music curriculum in recent years has created a 'have a go' culture and students at the school are happy to play instruments and sing with very little expertise but a great deal of enthusiasm. Working in partnership with the school's coaching team he has taken on the challenge of creating a song that can be used in a cross-phase workshop that reminds primary school students about the importance of phonics. To engage the older students he has chosen a variety of current pop songs, printed their lyrics and asked his Year 9 classes to rewrite them to include a rule from their phonics lessons as their main message. This is intended to be fun, yet in its execution the secondary school students have to remind themselves of their phonic knowledge and the primary school students get to see them produced in an entertaining fashion. One of the songs is 'Black Heart' by Stooshe (Warner Music UK, 2012). Tom played the students the original song and they instantly recognised it, singing along with gusto. He then played them a karaoke backing track version and announced that they had to rewrite the lyrics for a primary school audience, and would sing their version to this track. Their task was 'to keep them [the primary school students] interested in phonics'. The class were then given a brief reminder of the phonics currently displayed around school and had a discussion of ideas before the students went off to write their own version. This was then recorded in a following lesson in the school's small recording studio.

→

Part of the original lyrics:

Daddy I've fallen for a monster

Somehow he's scaring me half to death

He's big and he's bad

I love him like mad

Momma he's the best I've ever had

Daddy I've fallen for a monster

He got a black heart . . .

Part of the revised student lyrics:

Daddy I've fallen for the phonemes

But how they scare me half to death

There are lots and their sounds

Are hard to pronounce

But practice is making me announce

That Daddy I've fallen for the phonemes

They've got a good heart . . .

Tom was pleased that the Year 9 students had refreshed their own knowledge and the primary school students had a version of a song that kept phonics, and their importance, in their minds. He regularly sets this lesson with new songs and raps and the students look forward to being 'educational song writers'. He noticed that having a real purpose and a real audience for the task had given the project momentum and challenge.

There is considerable potential for engaging students with reading when links are made to their hobbies and interests. You will see more such links in Chapter 5, as well as below where football is the theme for a sound-matching activity.

Exploiting students' interest in football

Football's popularity means that it can offer opportunities to engage students who may show little interest in reading. Many who struggle to read manage to look at websites about their favourite teams, newspapers, football results and magazines. This interest could be capitalised upon in various ways and you might take advantage of the Football in the Community programmes which virtually all professional clubs run. Many clubs have education rooms and materials which include cross-curricular work and visits can be arranged.

At a simpler level, the development of phonological awareness can be made more interesting and engaging by using football teams and players as examples. You might try adapting a popular game into *football snap*.

Put team names in a hat and ask children to draw them out in turn and place them face up. When children place a team whose name includes the same phoneme as another on the table they call 'Snap' and have to explain which phoneme is the same. This can be played so that only phonemes with the same graphemes may count (e.g. Chel**s**ea and Swan**s**ea) or, for more advanced players, phonemes could be the same but represented by different graphemes too (e.g. Crystal Pala<u>c</u>e and A<u>s</u>ton V<u>i</u>lla). This game could be adapted to use names of TV programmes and personalities, singers, etc.

Alliteration

Challenge children to see how many words they can make which begin with the same grapheme/phoneme/group of letters. Alliterative phrases and sentences could focus on different themes based upon children's interests. For football, they might create alliterative headlines for sports pages (you could find some examples to show to them). For example:

> *Lucky Leicester lead lowly Liverpool.*
>
> *Delighted Doncaster dent Dagenham's dream.*

Challenges for teachers using a phonic approach

As you have seen in earlier chapters, the English alphabetic system has many inconsistencies, with most letters having more than one phoneme and it being possible to write most phonemes using different graphemes.

Many phonemes can be represented by more than one grapheme. For example, the k sound at the beginning of king can be made by ck at the end of kick, c in cat, cc in account, q in Iraq and ch in school. In the next chapter you will find an example of a spelling investigation involving children's names, but in the meantime look at examples of names found in three secondary schools. You will see that parents have chosen phonically plausible spellings for names which may differ from more common or traditional versions:

Kohnnerr, Connor, Conor, Konnor, Issak, Khyle, Kourtney, Kallum, Rachiel. There were also some 'invented' names, including *Kekezza, Shakonce, Nevaeh* (*Heaven* reversed) and *Jelisa*.

Activity 3.1   Grapheme variations

Look at the graphemes below and see how many alternative ways each can be represented, providing a word for each example. The first one has been done for you with some extra examples.

1. the sh sound in shop – ch in chef; ti- in station; ci- in optician

2. the f sound in fish

3. the j sound in jug

4. the n sound in not

5. the ee sound in feet

6. the ai sound in train

7. the ou sound in loud

8. the oo sound in food

9. the o sound in no

10. the schwa sound in the

(see Waugh and Harrison-Palmer, 2013)

Just as different graphemes can represent the same sound, many graphemes can be used for more than one phoneme. For example, *c* can be sounded differently in *cat* and *city*, *ch* can be sounded differently in *chip, chef* and *school*, and *o* is sounded differently in *no, not* and *woman*.

Activity 3.2   Phoneme variations

Look at the graphemes below and see how many alternative phonemes each can be used to represent, providing a word for each example. The first two have been done for you.

1. f – fog, of

2. g – gate, germ, regime

3. s

4. ou

5. ea

6. ow

7. y

8. ough

9. th

10. k

There are two further key challenges for teachers when supporting and developing children's phonic understanding: enunciation and discrimination between sounds.

Enunciation

This means to pronounce or articulate. It is important that we enunciate phonemes clearly and accurately when teaching children. This means avoiding adding additional sounds such as the *schwa* wherever possible. For many letters this is quite easy, for example, *f, l, m, n, r, s*, which should be sounded *fff, lll, mmm, nnn, rrr, sss* respectively. For some, however, it is difficult to avoid (b, d, t), but you should try to keep this as short as possible.

Look at the following, all of which were written by Key Stage 1 children and each of which represented a word in the children's writing:

cl   bt   jmp

Can you tell which words the children were trying to spell? In fact they were:

colour   butter   jumper

The children spelled them in what seemed to them to be a logical way because they, or perhaps they and their teachers, did not enunciate phonemes correctly. They had become used to hearing the hard c in cat sounded as 'cuh' with an added vowel sound, perhaps as you were when you learned the sounds made by letters, and the letter l as in log sounded as 'luh' rather than 'lll'. Consequently, when the children came to try to spell words they used the extra sound (or schwa) to replace a vowel. For butter, they knew buh and tuh, and for jumper they knew juh, muh, puh rather than j-u-mmm-p-er. A schwa is a short vowel sound such as we hear in words like *the, pencil, doctor* and *taken*. Say each of those words and notice the short sound made by the letters in bold: *the, pencil, doctor and taken*.

These examples show us the importance of correct enunciation of phonemes. We need to model this for the children we teach and it isn't difficult to do so. However, it is also important that we are aware of issues surrounding accents when we use a phonic approach. This can be a particular challenge where students' accents differ markedly from those of their teachers.

Discrimination between sounds

Look at the word *split*. How many phonemes (individual sounds) does it include? You may have decided, correctly, that it has five and can be segmented into /s/p/l/i/t/, but you may have segmented it as /spl/i/t/. Because you are an advanced and sophisticated reader, you are used to seeing the consonant cluster spl and perhaps thought that this was a single sound (try saying spl slowly and notice how your mouth makes three different shapes as you do so – each time your mouth makes a different shape you make a different sound or phoneme). Some people refer to consonant clusters such as spl as blends, but most modern phonics programmes refer to them as adjacent consonants.

Now look at some more words and segment them into graphemes:

crash   spout   flight

You should have segmented them as follows:

$$/c/r/a/sh/ \qquad /s/p/ou/t \qquad f/l/igh/t$$

Can you see that the *sh* sound in *crash* is made by the digraph /sh/; the *ou* in spout is a single sound (try saying *ou* and notice that your mouth doesn't change shape), and the *ie* sound in *flight* is made by the trigraph (three letters make one sound) /igh/.

Activity 3.3   Segmenting words

Look at the words below and segment them (the first two have been done for you).

clap	c	l	a	p
ship	sh	i	p	
scratch				
flood				
dream				
screech				
thrash				

Encouraging students to think about vocabulary
Calligrams

Calligrams are visual representations of a word that reflect its meaning. For example, the word *bridge* could be written in a curved shape like a hump-backed bridge, or the word bed could be written with the letters b and d enlarged to give the word the shape of a bed:

bed

Case study: Calligrams in PE

Within their PE classes Year 7 students need many different warm-up games and lesson starters. Wanting to create a physical warm-up game for her PE class, Nicola was keen to extend her students' knowledge of calligrams. She prepared a PowerPoint presentation of words that had a strong visual impact and, working in pairs and threes, the students had to quickly make a physical representation of the word. Just as the students knew that a calligram contains a visual image within it to aid instant understanding (for example, jagged writing like icicles to show the word 'ice'), they then had the opportunity to physically recreate these images in an amusing way. This embedded their phonic knowledge in a different way – they had to think about what the word was, what it meant, and how it could be 'written' and then made physical. This challenge was made increasingly difficult when the whole group had to 'become' or 'represent' the word. Importantly, this exercise did not take place in an English or even a Drama lesson: the message to students about literacy across all faculties has become loud and clear.

This lesson led to hilarious consequences and served as an excellent warm-up where the students were embedding their phonic knowledge while being prepared for a physical lesson. Nicola took photographs of the shapes and uploaded them before the end of the lesson. She then showed them to the class, who were asked if they thought that the physical representation of the word was indeed a 'calligram'. The students loved this and had some excellent ideas about how to improve the calligrams and make them more meaningful.

Work on calligrams can be extended to poetry, with whole lines or verses written in the shape of the subject being described: for example, curvy for a snake, or in the shape of a diamond or mountain.

Accents and phonics

Some secondary teachers may think that there is a complicated mystique about teaching phonics – there isn't. Once we have mastered a few very basic skills, supporting students can be quite simple. If we understand how words can be segmented into their individual phonemes and if we enunciate these phonemes accurately, we have the basic skills necessary. However, our enunciation can be affected by our accents.

Everyone has an individual accent: think how often you recognise a voice at the other end of the telephone without the caller even having to say his or her name. These accents can be grouped according to the areas where we live, so that we might refer to north-eastern accents, cockney accents or even 'posh' accents. In fact, there are variations in accents from town to town and so, for example, a Yorkshire accent will be quite different in Sheffield, Barnsley, Leeds, Hull and Harrogate.

Accent refers to phonological variations and should not be confused with dialect. All versions of a language are dialects and include words, phrases and clauses which may not appear in other dialects. Standard English is the dialect which is often accepted as 'correct' and is the version in which English should be written. However, Standard English may be spoken with any accent. Accent variation has been, and arguably still is, associated with variation in social classes (Trudgill, 2001). Accent is a key to a person's identity and any attempt to force an alternative accent on an individual is likely to result in reluctance, for it would imply the alteration of their persona (Walker, 2010). But why might accents present a problem when we teach reading?

Research focus: Accents

Teachers trying to alter how children speak or act can result in their becoming unmotivated, subsequently hindering their academic progress (Reyhner, 2008). Ogbu (1986) researched the 'academic disengagement' of ethnic minorities, noting that African American children can view teachers as enemies because they encourage them to 'act white' by teaching lessons which fail to reflect their language and culture. Consequently, standard phonics programmes are arguably unsuitable for these students (Fordham and Ogbu, 1986; Reyhner, 2008). An example of this occurs with African American speakers, who can be referred to as 'Ebonics' (Williams, 1975). 'Ebonics phonics' translates to mean 'black sounds', in reference to the grammar and pronunciation they use, which differs from 'Standard English'. Although these 'Ebonic features' of their language were markers of their identity, the Linguistic Society of America accepted that within larger society they would benefit from 'acquiring Standard English' (Rickford, 1997). Experimental evidence suggested this might be better achieved within schools if approaches took 'ebonic features' into account as conventional approaches had shown little success.

Phonics schemes in England are designed on the basis of an attempted 'neutral' accent, usually referred to as Received Pronunciation (RP). In the past this *accent* has also been described as 'the Queen's English' or 'BBC English'; an accent associated with the highest status, which has 'no regional features' (Honeybone and Watson, 2006). However, it is now speculated that only three per cent of the British speakers of English speak in the form of this Received Pronunciation, with the majority of people in Britain speaking in the accent associated with their region (Jenkins, 2002). Although only a minority use Received Pronunciation, phonics schemes are designed with the grapheme–phoneme correspondences of their 'accent' (Honeybone and Watson, 2006). *Phonics International* suggests that there are around 44 phonemes in the spoken English language, but this statistic is specific to Received Pronunciation (Hepplewhite, 2007).

Accents can have a different number of phonemes, resulting in the phonemic contrasts (Roach, 2000: 209). For example, in Manchester there would be no distinction between the phonemes /oo/ and /u/ for they have no /u/ in their vowel system, unlike RP. Meaning, when a person with the regional accent of Manchester says *but* and *good*, the phonemes would be b/oo/t and g/oo/d, showing no clear distinction between the graphemes /u/ and /oo/ (Barry, 2006). Therefore, the grapheme–phoneme correspondences differ from that of RP, which could cause confusion if they are being taught by programmes that are based on RP pronunciation (Honeybone and Watson, 2006). One could argue that similarly to the African American speakers, students who do not speak 'the Queen's English' might respond negatively to the teaching of grapheme–phoneme correspondences which do not reflect their language and culture.

Trainee teachers in the north-east have reported that in some schools they are instructed to use the local accent when teaching phonics. For example, in some schools situated in areas where book, look, and took are pronounced with a long vowel sound for oo as in boot and shoot, trainees are expected to teach the *oo* grapheme as a consistently long vowel digraph. Trainees also report that where the local accent pronounces sure and pure to rhyme with *brewer* and *skewer*, children are taught that –*ure*, which is a single phoneme in most parts of England is sounded as two sounds (although the sound is taught as a single phoneme).

In southern England, words like *grass, bath* and *pass* tend to be pronounced with a long *aa* sound. For southern teachers working in the north and northerners teaching in the south, this can lead to confusion for children, and some trainees have found children adding an *r* when spelling some words because of their teacher's accent *(barth, parth, farst)*. This might be thought to be less of a problem now than, say, 50 years ago, because people all over the country are familiar with regional accents and understand some of the differences because of television programmes such as *EastEnders, Coronation Street, Emmerdale* and *Vera*.

Activity 3.4

Should teachers pronounce phonemes as the children do; as they would themselves; or as phonics programmes suggest?

Research focus: Linguistic phonics

A new phonics method was piloted in Belfast during 2004: Linguistic Phonics. The approach focuses on establishing a relationship between the children's spoken and written language; using children's native speech sounds and 'marrying the sounds' with written words (Gray *et al.*, 2006). Regarding the children's accent, they are given the opportunity to 'build *their* knowledge' as they will use phonemes in a context that makes sense to them (Gray *et al.*, 2006). Through these experiences with language, children will alter their structure of understanding (Vygotsky, 1980) and eventually learn to read and write. The Linguistic Phonics trial involved 22 schools and resulted in an improvement in reading standards, especially for low-ability reading groups. Parents also reported that the students enjoyed reading more, while post-primary schools noted a positive effect on both students' written work and their self-esteem (Belfast Education and Library Board, 2004).

However, linguistic phonics is not the only strategy being implemented in the UK to overcome the issue of accent variation. The Linguists Association of GB (LAGB) in 2006 discussed how professional phoneticians could support schools by creating tables that highlight phoneme–grapheme correspondences of specific regions or cities (Barry, 2006). This would allow teachers to use the systematic synthetic phonics approach, while avoiding confusion which could arise from materials designed for RP (Honeybone and Watson, 2006). To date, there have been 'accent guides' published for Liverpool (Honeybone and Watson, 2006), Manchester (Barry, 2003) and Newcastle (Watt, 2003). This approach is accent-specific, unlike linguistic phonics. However, adapting the approach to the local area makes it more likely to reflect the accent and culture of the children attending school. There is a limited amount of evidence to prove the effectiveness of accent guides, and they have only been published for three cities, with the most recent being six years ago, so there will need to be more research before the strategy becomes widely used.

Students with specific learning difficulties in reading

Consider for a moment a student in Year 7 who finds reading challenging. He may already have been diagnosed as having a specific learning difficulty such as dyslexia. In secondary school many teachers will meet the student and not all may be aware of his needs in the same way. He may be branded lazy or be criticised for work which is regarded as unsatisfactory, but which may represent his best efforts. He may have looked forward to secondary school as a fresh start after years of struggling at primary school, but he will quickly become disillusioned if his difficulties are not recognised and addressed. As the Rose Review maintained:

> it is well known that the nature of the problems for secondary aged children who have experienced repeated failure with reading often include negative attitudes and disengagement that are much more entrenched than in primary schools. Additional support for those children starting secondary school without secure reading skills is essential if they are to make progress and not fall further behind their peers.

(DCSF, 2009, p. 13)

Students with difficulties will find problems with textbooks, websites and worksheets. They may be reluctant or unable to read to the class. They may not be able to read instructions. They may not be able to read timetables and notices. Their specific problems may include:

- lack of phonic knowledge;
- lack of word attack strategies;
- lack of idea about semantic clues;
- lack of appreciation of the value and importance of reading;
- lack of confidence.

Since reading, writing, and speaking and listening permeate the curricula of most subjects, teachers of all subjects need to be teachers of English (particularly since the introduction of penalties for poor spelling and grammar in public examinations). Teachers also need to be aware that many students may demonstrate symptoms of dyslexia. The Rose Review (2009: 29) provides the following working definition of dyslexia.

- **Dyslexia is a learning difficulty that primarily affects the skills involved in accurate and fluent word reading and spelling.**

- Characteristic features of dyslexia are difficulties in phonological awareness, verbal memory and verbal processing speed.

- Dyslexia occurs across the range of intellectual abilities.

- It is best thought of as a continuum, not a distinct category, and there are no clear cut-off points.

- Co-occurring difficulties may be seen in aspects of language, motor co-ordination, mental calculation, concentration and personal organisation, but these are not, by themselves, markers of dyslexia.

- A good indication of the severity and persistence of dyslexic difficulties can be gained by examining how the individual responds or has responded to well-founded intervention.

It is important that all teachers recognise the challenges which students with dyslexia and other learning difficulties face and cater for their needs. This knowledge and understanding, allied to strategies, can actually benefit other students too, as Riddick maintained.

An argument put forward by both Swansea LEA and the BDA (British Dyslexia Association) is that many of the practices advocated for a dyslexia friendly school will benefit a wide range of children and not just those children identified as having dyslexia.

(Riddick, 2006: 146)

Research focus: Asking dyslexic children about dyslexic-friendly teaching

Riddick states that:

If word-level difficulties in fluent and accurate word reading and spelling are central to the definition of dyslexia, dyslexia friendly practices should encompass a specific focus on helping children with special needs address such difficulties directly.

(Riddick, 2006: 142)

→

Riddick (1995, 1996) and Johnson (2004) asked students to think about the character-istics of teachers who made learning easy and those who made it difficult for them. Students were asked always to think about teachers, classes and schools in their own experience. The results, which Riddick combined and summarised, can be seen in the table below. Responses from primary and secondary students were similar but there were some interesting differences.

Good teachers	Poor teachers
Primary and secondary items	*Primary items*
• kind and helpful • patient and approachable • explain things clearly and will re-explain • do not embarrass or humiliate • do not shout when you get things wrong • write things down clearly and leave on view • happy to answer questions • understand your learning difference	• shout a lot • do not give time to copy things down • angry if we do not understand • humiliate in front of class, e.g. ask for test scores in public *Secondary items additional to above* • unwilling to answer questions • make us read out loud in front of class • too much copying from the board • ignore or undervalue • put in bottom sets • mark down for poor spelling, grammar or handwriting

Source: Riddick, 2006: 149.

Activity 3.5

Think about the students' responses above and relate this to your own prac-tice (or practice you have observed). Has your practice (or practice observed) been 'dyslexia-friendly' or could lessons have been improved?

To find out more about strategies to support children with dyslexia, see the Rose Review (2009), but the following simple strategies offer a good starting point.

• Highlight and discuss new subject vocabulary.

• Provide differentiated reading materials to cater for students who would not cope with some texts.

• Use visual clues such as pictures, charts and diagrams to support reading.

• Teach students how to highlight key words in texts.

• Check that students understand what they need to do and what they have read.

• Use IT where appropriate to provide a different medium of text.

More strategies to meet the challenges

Use speaking and listening to develop subject learning

This book is chiefly concerned with the development of children's reading, but it is important to understand that if reading is a barrier to learning across the curriculum for some children we must find other strategies to give them access to that curriculum while addressing their literacy skills. This may involve ensuring that there is always a strong oral element to teaching, especially where students need to follow instruction or extract information from text. Many students can understand concepts in subjects such as mathematics, geography and science when they are carefully explained orally or through illustrations, but are unable to develop their understanding when their weak reading skills present a barrier to learning.

Many secondary teachers make extensive use of digital resources, including video, to enable children to see processes in action. When these accompany written information, children will have more strategies for understanding, especially semantic approaches which help us to acquire meaning from text. Think back to your experience of children's TV – programmes for very young children enable them to develop an understanding of the world around them through pictures and cartoons. It is only later that these may include written vocabulary.

Link reading to writing

Not only are students expected to read subject-related texts, but they are also expected to write in different ways in different subjects. For example, writing up experiments in science, writing discursive essays in English and history, producing descriptions of cycles and information about places in geography, and writing instruction in design technology. If students are to write in an appropriate style, it is important that the process and style is modelled for them by their teachers. Shared writing involves the teacher acting as a scribe to write while the class watches and listens to his or her thought processes spoken aloud, followed by the teacher scribing using the students' suggestions.

By modelling writing in this way we can address students' misconceptions and give them a platform for success. We can also address issues around phrasing, vocabulary and spelling, perhaps creating word banks as we write so that these can be used as a reference point when students work independently or in small groups.

Engage students with new and subject-specific vocabulary

As students start Year 7, they meet new vocabulary associated with around ten or 11 subjects, as well as with school life. Perhaps you can recall similar experiences in your own education where some people used terms with which you were unfamiliar. Think about starting higher education when terms you may have met can include acronyms such as JCR, SU and words like seminar, tutorial, fresher, and refectory. When you met these terms you were already a successful reader with a wide vocabulary, but for Year 7 children, especially those whose reading may be weak, new terms can be challenging and even alienating. This is particularly so when there are also unfamiliar grapheme representations of phonemes. For example, *puy, avalanche, crevice, precipice* are all geographical terms they might encounter in Year 7.

Case study: A year-group approach to vocabulary development

Sarah, a geography teacher in a seven-form-entry rural comprehensive school, made use of classroom displays of illustrations accompanying key vocabulary. She showed through the displays and discussions with her classes that many geographical terms also related to words used in other subjects: for example, geo (geometry, geography, geology, geode); hydro (hydraulic, hydrate, dehydrate); urban (suburban, urbane). Sarah found that students were interested in links, and this was commented upon by the head of Year 7, who had noticed that students in her maths classes appeared knowledgeable about terms such as *geometry* and *geometric*.

At a Year 7 team meeting it was suggested that all members of staff should provide short lists of key vocabulary, with brief definitions, which students would encounter in their subjects each term, and these should be combined into a glossary to be given to each student. At a subsequent meeting, staff discussed links between terms used in different subjects and strategies for supporting students' spelling and understanding of the words.

The vocabulary lists were developed into short leaflets which could be provided for parents, both to keep them informed about what their children were studying and to enable them to support their children with homework.

In Chapter 4 you will find another example of subject teams working together to support children's spelling of the vocabulary they need to use. Try Activity 3.6 to consider how you could support students in your school.

Activity 3.6   Supporting students in learning vocabulary

Children might come across the words below in Year 7:

archaeology (in history); *bisect* (in mathematics); *les mains* (in French); *urbanisation* (in geography); *centrifugal* (in science).

What strategies could you use to help them to pronounce and understand these words? Once you have noted some initial ideas, look at the next section for further strategies.

Further strategies for supporting vocabulary development

The strategies below have all been observed in secondary schools and could easily be incorporated into work in your subject.

Create word banks

When you are introducing writing activities, write key vocabulary on the board or on pieces of card which can later be placed in alphabetical order as a reference point. This will not only help students to spell more accurately, but it will also provide prompts to help their composition.

Make word and definition cards

Use words from your word bank and discuss their meanings. Write definitions on separate pieces of card and use the word cards and the definition cards for a matching/snap activity which will help reinforce students' understanding of the vocabulary.

Create glossaries

Use word and definition cards to create subject- or topic-specific glossaries as an alphabetical reference point. These glossaries can be used as revision aids at examination times.

Display word cluster posters

Draw students' attention to the common letter patterns and morphemes in words. Explain their meanings and ask students to create word clusters for display in subject rooms; for example, *equal, equalise, equate, equilateral, equality, equation, equidistant, equilibrium*). Point out their common root (*equal/equi*, from the Latin word meaning *to make even*) and how that helps with both spelling and meaning.

In this chapter you have seen examples of some of the challenges which teachers face when developing students' literacy skills in secondary schools. You have also seen strategies which can be used across the curriculum to enable students to engage with subjects and develop an understanding of subject-specific vocabulary. In each of the first three chapters you have seen how the English alphabetic code presents challenges because of its many irregularities and the various accents which teachers and students use, and have looked at ways of developing your own subject knowledge. In the next chapter you will see how you can support students' spelling development.

Activities: answers and discussion

Activity 3.1   Grapheme variations

You were asked to look at the graphemes below and see how many alternative ways each can be represented, providing a word for each example. Your answers might include:

1. the sh sound in shop – ch in chef; ci in delicious; ti in nation

2. the f sound in fish – ph in photograph; gh in laugh; ff in off

3. the j sound in jug – g in gem; dge in edge

4. the n sound in not – gn in gnat; kn in knit; pn in pneumatic; nn in dinner

5. the ee sound in feet – ea in read; ei in receive; ie in grief; e-e in eve

6. the ai sound in train – ay in day; eigh in weigh; ey in grey

7. the ou sound in loud – ow in now; ough in bough

8. the oo sound in food – ew in threw; ough in through; u-e in rude

9. the o sound in no – ow in know; oa in coat; o-e in nose

10. the schwa sound in the – a in woman or in doctor; er in teacher

Activity 3.2   Phoneme variations

You were asked to look at the graphemes and see how many alternative phonemes each can be used to represent, providing a word for each example. You can see some possibilities below, but you probably found more:

1. f   fat, of

2. g   get, germ, gnat

3. s   sit, is, sugar

4. ou   noun, cough, tough

5. ea   head, meat, steak, idea, earth

6. ow   now, know

7. y   you, by, easy

8. ough tough, bough, bought, through, though

9. th   this, think

10. k   kick, know

Activity 3.3   Segmenting words

clap	c	l	a	p	
ship	sh	i	p		
scratch	s	c	r	a	tch
flood	f	l	oo	d	
dream	d	r	ea	m	
screech	s	c	r	ee	ch
thrash	th	r	a	sh	

Websites which will help you develop your phonic skills

There are several useful websites where you can find examples of blending and segmenting and watch videos of teachers at work. These include:

Mr Thorne Does Phonics, available at: www.mrthorne.com/

Sonic Phonics (2011), available at www.talkingproducts.com/sonic-phonics.html (accessed 16 March 2012)

Further reading

For fascinating insights into regional accents and for maps showing how words are pronounced differently in different areas:
British Library (n.d.) *Phonological variation,* retrieved November 2013 from: www.bl.uk/learning/langlit/sounds/regional-voices/phonological-variation/

For guidance on teaching phonics:
Jolliffe, W. and Waugh, D. with Carss, A. (2012) *Teaching systematic synthetic phonics in primary schools*. London: Sage.

McGuinness, D. (2004) *Early reading instruction: What science really tells us about how to teach reading*. Cambridge, MA: MIT Press.

For guidance on dyslexia:
DCSF (2009*) Identifying and teaching children and young people with dyslexia and literacy difficulties: An independent report from Sir Jim Rose to the Secretary of State for Children, Schools and Families*. Nottingham: DCSF.

References

Barry, S. (2003*) Phoneme–grapheme correspondences and a Manchester accent*. Education Committee of the Linguistics Association of Great Britain, available at: www.phon.ucl. ac.uk/home/dick/ec/accents.htm

Barry S. M. E. (2006) *Accents and phonics: How can linguists help?* Newcastle, UK: LAGB 2006 Linguistics in Education. Retrieved November 2013 from: ftp://ftp.phon.ucl. ac.uk/pub/Word-Grammar/ec/barry.pdf

Belfast Education and Library Board (n.d.) *Linguistic phonics*. Retrieved November 2013 from: www.belb.org.uk/parents/literacy_linguistic.asp?sm=37

DCSF (2009*) Identifying and teaching children and young people with dyslexia and literacy difficulties: An independent report from Sir Jim Rose to the Secretary of State for Children, Schools and Families*. Nottingham: DCSF.

DfES (2000) *Progression in phonics: Materials for whole-class teaching* (4419). Retrieved from DfES website: http://dera.ioe.ac.uk/4419/

Fordham, S. and Ogbu, J. U. (1986) Black students' school success: Coping with the 'burden of "acting white"'. *The urban review*, 18 (3): 176–206.

Gray, C., Behan, S., Dunbar, C., Dunn, J., Ferguson, J. and Mitchell, D. (2006) The impact of the linguistic phonics approach on children's reading, writing and spelling. First published for the Belfast Education and Library Board in 2006 by The Stranmillis Press (an imprint of Stranmillis University College, Belfast BT9 5DY).

Hepplewhite, D. (2007) International online synthetic phonics programme. Retrieved from Phonics International website: www.phonicsinternational.com/guidance_book. pdf (last accessed 26 September 2013).

Honeybone, P. and Watson, K. (2006) *Phonemes, graphemes and phonics for Liverpool English*. Education Committee of the Linguistics Association of Great Britain. Downloadable from: www.phon.ucl. ac.uk/home/dick/ec/accents.htm

Jenkins, J. (2002) A sociolinguistically based, empirically researched pronunciation syllabus for English as an international language. *Applied Linguistics,* 23 (1): 83–103.

Johnson, M. (2004) Dyslexia friendly schools – policy and practice, in Reid, G. and Fawcett, A. (eds) *Dyslexia in context*. London: Whurr Publishers, pp. 237–56.

Reyhner, J. (2008) The reading wars: Phonics versus whole language. Unpublished manuscript. Arizona, USA: Department of Educational Specialties, Northern Arizona University. Retrieved from: http://jan.ucc.nau.edu/~jar/Reading_Wars.html

Rickford, J. R. (1997) Suite for ebony and phonics. *Discover*, 18 (12): 82–7.

Riddick, B. (1995) Dyslexia and development: An interview study. *Dyslexia*, 1 (2): 63–74.

Riddick, B. (1996) *Living with dyslexia: The social and emotional consequences of specific learning difficulties.* London: Routledge.

Riddick, B. (2006) Dyslexia friendly schools in the UK. *Topics in Language Disorders*, 26 (2): 142–54.

Roach, P. (2000) *English phonetics and phonology.* 3rd edition. Cambridge: Cambridge University Press, p. 209.

Trudgill, P. (2001) The sociolinguistics of modern RP, in Trudgill, P., *Sociolinguistic variation and change.* Edinburgh: Edinburgh University Press, pp. 176–8.

Vygotsky, L. S. (1980) *Mind in society: The development of higher psychological processes.* Harvard University Press, p. 216.

Walker, R. (2010) *Teaching the pronunciation of English as a lingua franca.* Oxford: Oxford University Press.

Watt, D. (2003) *Phoneme–grapheme correspondences and a Newcastle accent.* Education Committee of the Linguistics Association of Great Britain. Retrieved from: www.phon.ucl.ac.uk/home/dick/ec/accents.htm

Waugh, D. and Harrison-Palmer, R. (2013) *Teaching systematic synthetic phonics: Audit and Test.* London: Sage.

Williams, R. (1975) *Ebonics: The true language of black folks.* St Louis: Institute of Black Studies.

4 Phonics into spelling (morphology and spelling strategies)

Learning outcomes

By reading this chapter you will develop:

- an understanding of some of the challenges of teaching and learning English spellings;
- an appreciation of some strategies for teaching and learning spelling;
- an understanding of key aspects of spelling, including spelling rules and generalisations, morphemes, grapheme–phoneme correspondences and homophones and homographs;
- an awareness of some possibilities for studying spelling across the curriculum.

2012 Teachers' Standards

2. Promote good progress and outcomes by pupils:

- demonstrate knowledge and understanding of how pupils learn and how this impacts on teaching.

3. Demonstrate good subject and curriculum knowledge:

- have a secure knowledge of the relevant subject(s) and curriculum areas, foster and maintain pupils' interest in the subject, and address misunderstandings;
- demonstrate an understanding of and take responsibility for promoting high standards of literacy, articulacy and the correct use of Standard English, whatever the teacher's specialist subject.

Before you read this chapter, try Activity 4.1 below.

Activity 4.1   The /k/ sound

Whenever people want to demonstrate how to spell words phonically they seem to give *cat (c/a/t/)* as their example. The initial letter in cat makes a /k/ sound in the same way that *k* makes a /k/ sound in *kick*. How many ways can you represent the /k/ sound in English? The graphemes you choose may appear anywhere in words and do not necessarily have to be only those which can begin words.

You probably came up with some or all of the following: *ck* as in *lock*, *cc* as in *account*, *c* as in *coat*, *k* as in *kind*, *ch* as in *school* and *q* as in *Iraq*. This simple activity illustrates how challenging it can be to make correct spelling choices. Clearly, we need strategies to help us and these are described in this chapter.

Introduction

As you have seen in earlier chapters, English is a difficult language to learn to read and spell because it has 26 letters, but around 44 phonemes and well over 200 ways of spelling the 44 phonemes. Compare this with many other languages such as Finnish and Italian which have fewer phonemes, almost all of which are always represented by the same letters (graphemes), and it can be seen that English speakers face a much greater challenge when learning to read and write than many other nationalities (see Chapter 2).

Cossu *et al.* (1995) found that young Italian readers achieve 92 per cent accuracy on word reading tests after just six months of tuition. Spencer (2002) found that most students in the lowest ability group in Year 2 could successfully spell words using the simple alphabetic code, but that mastering the most difficult common words required an additional three years of schooling.

Given the problems associated with the English alphabetic code, it might be argued that teaching reading and spelling using a phonic approach is inappropriate. However, according to Crystal (2009) the average adult is likely to have a vocabulary of 35–50,000 words. Even if everyone learned to spell 20 new words each week for the 12 years spent in school, only around 8,000 would be learned. We can't learn each word by rote, so we need strategies we can apply and generalisations about spelling patterns. And despite our complex alphabetic code, there are many things we can generalise about, even if some generalisations cannot be turned into rules which have no exceptions. An understanding of the relationship between letters and sounds (graphemes and phonemes) is essential if we are to have any idea about the spelling possibilities for a new word. Indeed, Crystal (2005) maintains that only around 400 words are so unpredictable they need to be learned by rote, so strategies can be devised to learn most words in English.

Research focus: Rimes

One of the notable features of the patterns contained in the English written language is that the parts of words known as rimes contain stable spellings and stable pronunciations. Rimes are parts of words that are spelt the same way, so that in a word such as 'cake' the rime is 'ake' and the initial consonant or consonants are called the onset of the word. The use of onset and rime, largely derived from the work of Goswami (1995), became very popular as the focus for teaching reading. This approach is what is termed 'analytic phonics', where words are decoded based on shared patterns with other words. As a method of teaching reading this has drawbacks in not teaching systematically all 44-plus phonemes and their alternative spellings and pronunciations. However, where this has real value is in teaching spelling. The table below provides a list of 37 rimes that provide nearly 500 words in English.

$\longrightarrow$

Table 4.1 *37 rimes that provide nearly 500 English words*

-ack	-ain	-ake	-ale	-all	-ame	-an	-ank
-ap	-ash	-at	-ate	-aw	-ay	-eat	-ell
-est	-ice	-ick	-ide	-ite	-ill	-in	-ine
-ing	-ink	-ip	-ir	-ock	-oke	-op	-or
-ore	-uck	-ug	-ump	-unk			

Source: Wylie and Durrell, 1970: 787–91.

It is therefore helpful for spelling to learn long vowel phonemes accompanied with teaching of spelling patterns. Research has shown that the brain is a competent pattern detector and when a pattern is detected in a word, it evokes associations; for example, a word like *complaint* may be associated with mail, paint and constraint (Ehri, 2005).

We all make use of phonic strategies to read and spell new words, either looking at each letter, digraph or trigraph and assigning a phoneme to it or grouping sounds into syllables to break a word into manageable chunks. Try Activity 4.2 below to see how you deal with words you have never seen before.

Activity 4.2   Reading pseudo-words

Try reading each of the words below. Think carefully about how you approach each word.

brindinisation

disjastifying

clamdidliocious

Try reading the words to colleagues and ask them to attempt to spell them. Do they segment the word into sounds or syllables? Do they ask you to repeat the word slowly so that they can do this? How close are their spellings to the versions above?

You probably found that your colleagues were very close to writing the words as shown above, because they are familiar with the relationship between phonemes and graphemes, even if they were never formally taught phonics.

Frith (1985) argued that once children start to segment the phonemes when they write, they become more fluent as writers and their spelling begins to develop. So it is important that we continue to focus on letter–sound correspondences beyond the primary school. This approach is valuable even for more advanced readers and writers when they meet unfamiliar grapheme–phoneme correspondences, and it is vital for those children whose phonemic awareness is less well developed.

Research focus: Why can spelling be so difficult?

Crystal (2005) maintains that many people who read well find spelling difficult, although there are people who are able to spell words which they find hard to read. He states that *more things can go wrong while spelling: there are far more graphemic alternatives for a phoneme than there are phonemic alternatives for a grapheme* (p.129). Crystal gives the example of beat which can only really have one possible pronunciation, but when the word is given orally there are several alternative ways in which it could be written – *beet, beate, beete, biet* and *beat*. According to Crystal, *one study worked out that there are 13.7 spellings per sound in English, but only 3.5 sounds per letter.*

The history of English explains some of its irregularities. Crystal described how in the Anglo-Saxon period English had an alphabet of 24 graphemes (the Latin alphabet plus four new symbols) but the language had nearly 40 phonemes. This meant that to make some sounds letters had to be combined. This continues today and many words include digraphs (*ship, heap, out*), trigraphs (*high, match*) and even quadgraphs (*though, sleigh*).

After the Norman Conquest some words were spelled in a more French way, with *qu* replacing *cw* (*queen*) and *c* replacing *s* in words like *circle* and *cell*.

Early printers were often foreign and used the spelling norms of their home language when printing. The language also changed in pronunciation, with vowels being sounded differently from the fifteenth century and some letters which were sounded in Anglo-Saxon becoming silent – the letter k in *knight, kneel* etc.

Later, some spellings were modified and letters were added to show words' Latin or Greek roots – debt acquired its silent b to show that it came from the Latin *debitum*, for example. English has continued to acquire words from other languages and their spellings; for example, *pizza, picturesque, jodhpurs, muesli*.

Crystal concludes:

> *The result is a 'system' that is an amalgam of Anglo-Saxon, French, Classical and other sources. The system is basically a phonemic one, but the phonemes are represented by letter patterns as well as single letters. As a result, the task facing the child learner is much greater than in the case of a system (such as Spanish and Welsh) where for the most part there is a regular one sound-one spelling relationship throughout.*
>
> (Crystal, 2005: 131)

All of these developments have left us with inconsistencies and irregularities which mean that even some of our most common words have irregularities or might be termed 'tricky' at some stages of children's literacy development. *Letters and Sounds* (DfES, 2007) lists as 'tricky' a selection of words taken from the 100 most common words in English. These are shown in Table 4.2 below.

Table 4.2   Some common tricky words

the	me	said	little	Mrs
to	be	have	one	looked
I	was	like	when	called
no	you	so	out	asked
go	they	do	what	could
into	all	some	oh	
he	are	come	their	
she	my	were	people	
we	her	there	Mr	

Source: DfES (2007) Letters and Sounds. London: DfES.

You may well have looked at the words above and thought that most were very straightforward, but for children coming to terms with reading and writing it must be difficult, for instance, to understand that in *to, do* and *no* the vowel sounds are different, while **they** will find very few other words in which the /ai/ sound is represented by *ey*. Look at *was* and consider why people might spell it 'woz'; and what about *were* and *there*; and *people*? These common words form the bulk of the vocabulary found in texts, so it is vital that students are supported to learn to read and spell them. As the National Strategies found:

> *Students sometimes misspell common words because they have spelt those words incorrectly for a long time and now have the pattern for that incorrect spelling in their hand and eye. We need to encourage them to look afresh at these words and re-learn them correctly.*

(DCSF, 2010a: 15)

A simple strategy for your classroom could be to display the most common words prominently as a reference point for students, perhaps alongside a display of key vocabulary associated with their current learning in your subject.

Teaching students how to learn spellings

A key element in any spelling programme or whole-school strategy is to show children how to learn spellings. There are still teachers who think that they have taught spelling if they have given children lists of words to learn for a test. This alone is not teaching spelling, especially if it is not accompanied by discussions about the words to be learned and strategies for learning them. It is important to discuss phoneme– grapheme correspondences in context, as in the case study below. A good way to get students to think about spelling and letter–sound correspondences is to ask them to focus on people's names and the different ways in which they are spelled and the many ways in which they could possibly be spelled. You will find many examples of alternative spellings among your students and it can be challenging for teachers when writing reports to use the right spelling for the right student, especially when you may teach several children whose names sound the same, but are spelled in different ways.

Case study: Spelling investigations: spelling names

Katherine, an English teacher in a suburban academy, noticed that she taught several girls who shared her first name, but that their names were spelled in several different ways. She decided to set her lower sets in Year 7 the task of working out spelling possibilities for the name, giving them homework to find the names of as many famous *Katherines* (whatever the spelling) as they could. The teacher wanted students to think carefully about the ways in which the sounds in the name can be represented and intended to follow up the activity with similar ones related to other names.

Katherine introduced the activity towards the end of a lesson and began by asking students to segment *Katherine* into phonemes. There was some debate about whether it should be /k/a/th/er/i/ne/ or /k/a/th/r/i/ne, but it was agreed that there were six phonemes in the name regardless of how it was pronounced. She then asked them to work in pairs to find at least three phonically plausible alternative spellings. In the short time available, the class came up with:

Cathrine, Catherine, Cathryn, Kathryn, Cathrin and Kathrin.

By the time of their next lesson many students had found the names of famous Katherines as well as those of fellow students and the list now included:

Kathrine, Cathrine, Kathryn, Cathryn, Kathrynn, Cathrynn, Katherin, Catherin, Kathrin, Cathrin, Katherine, Catherine, Katheryn, Catheryn, Katherynn, Catherynn, Chathrine, Chathryn, Chathrin, Chatherine, Chatheryn, Chatherin, Chatherynn, Katharine, Katharin, Katharyn, Katharynn, Catharine, Catharin, Catharyn, Catharynn, Chatharine, Chatharin, Chatharyn, Chatharynn, Kathryne, Cathryne, Chathryne, Katheryne, Catheryne, Chatheryne, Katharyne, Catharyne, Chatharyne, Kathrynne, Cathrynne, Chathrynne, Katherynne, Catherynne, Chatherynne, Katharynne, Catharynne, Chatharynne, Kathren, Cathren, Chathren, Katheren, Catheren, Chatheren, Katharen, Catharen, Chatharen, Kathrenn, Cathrenn, Chathrenn, Katherenn, Catherenn, Chatherenn, Katharenn

Katherine wrote every spelling suggested on the board and encouraged the class to question the spellings, and asked those who provided them to justify them. The first version which began with 'ch' was queried immediately, but the students who had included this spelling pointed out that several words begin with ch and are sounded with a hard /k/ sound, for example, *choir, chemist* and *chord.*

$\longrightarrow$

The activity was a great success in getting students to think carefully about grapheme–phoneme correspondences and possibilities. It led to explorations of the origins of names and how these might justify certain spellings and of the most common versions. Students went on to look at other names, starting with their own and those of their favourite celebrities, and created as many alternative plausible spellings as possible.

Activity 4.3   Developing spelling investigations

Katherine's classes were also set the challenge of finding any names which could only have one possible spelling. Can you think of any first names which could only be spelled in one possible way? You might start with short, phonically regular names such as *Ben*, *Sam*, *Tom*, *Pat* and *Jade*: can you find alternative spellings for these?

How could you develop similar spelling investigations in your own subject areas?

National Curriculum links

We still need to use phonic strategies when we meet new words, even as adults. For students beginning to study a range of subjects at secondary school, new vocabulary can be daunting and sometimes difficult to spell and read. Look at the extracts from the National Curriculum (DfE, 2013) and note the emphasis on vocabulary and a knowledge of subject-specific terminology.

In science:

> *Students should develop their use of scientific vocabulary, including the use of scientific nomenclature and units and mathematical representations.* (p. 187)

In geography:

> *physical geography relating to: geological timescales and plate tectonics; rocks, weathering and soils; weather and climate, including the change in climate from the Ice Age to the present; and glaciation, hydrology and coasts;*

> *human geography relating to: population and urbanisation; international development; economic activity in the primary, secondary, tertiary and quaternary sectors; and the use of natural resources.* (p. 217)

In history:

> *They should use historical terms and concepts in increasingly sophisticated ways.* (p. 223)

It is clear that some of the above vocabulary will present challenges for students who will be expected not only to understand the terms but also to spell them accurately.

Spelling rules

The solution often provided to learning to spell is to learn spelling rules. Most people, when asked to name a spelling rule, offer '*i* before *e*, except after *c*', and many are at a loss to think of any others. Judy Parkinson's (2007) entertaining book, *i before e (except after c)*, looks at what the subtitle calls 'old-school ways to remember stuff'. Interestingly, the chapter on spelling focuses almost entirely on mnemonics for remembering spellings and the only 'rule' examined in any detail is *i before e except after c*, which Parkinson shows has so many exceptions that it requires several additions if it is to be reasonably accurate. Parkinson (2007: 21) ends up with:

> *i* before *e*, except after *c*
>
> or when sounded like *a*
>
> as in *neighbour* and *weigh*
>
> drop this rule when -*c* sounds as *sh*.

You might feel that the 'rule' is pretty well discredited by the time those additions have been made, and it is unlikely that it will trip off the tongue and be remembered in the same way as the inaccurate but catchily rhyming *i* before *e*, except after *c*.

Why is i before e not a very good spelling rule?

There are so many exceptions to the 'rule' that it can be both confusing and misleading. These exceptions include:

> *ancient, beige, being, codeine, conscience, deify, deity, deign, eider, eight, either, feign, feint, feisty, foreign, forfeit, freight, heifer, height, heinous, heir, heist, neigh, neighbour, neither, prescient, rein, reign, reinvest, reignite, science, seeing, seismic, seize, sheik, society, sovereign, surfeit, their, veil, vein, weight, weir, weird*

What are the characteristics of a good spelling rule?

Spelling patterns, rather than rules, are discussed by O'Sullivan and Thomas (2007) who emphasise the importance of analogy. The National Curriculum (2013) refers to *rules and generalisations*. What is clear is that there are spelling conventions and guidelines that actually work in most cases. For a rule or spelling generalisation to be useful it needs to work consistently and have very few if any exceptions. *Support for Spelling* (DSCF, 2010a) provides excellent guidance on spelling generalisations.

This very useful publication is no longer in print, but can be found online. Look at the extracts below and see how they could be used to support students' spelling development and understanding of spelling probabilities.

Position of phonemes

*The **ai** and **oi** spellings do not occur at the end of English words or immediately before suffixes; instead, the **ay** and **oy** spellings are used in these positions (e.g. play, played, playing, playful, joy, joyful, enjoying, enjoyment). In other positions, the /ai/ sound is most often spelt **ai** or a consonant-vowel, as in rain, date and bacon. The same principle applies in choosing between **oi** and **oy**: oy is used at the end of a word or immediately before a suffix, and **oi** is used elsewhere. There is no other spelling for this phoneme.*

O sound following a w sound

*When an /o/ sound follows a /w/ sound, it is frequently spelt with the letter **a** (e.g. was, wallet, want, wash, watch, wander) – often known as the **w special**. This extends to many words where the /w/ sound comes from the **qu** grapheme (e.g. quarrel, quantity, squad, squash).*

Ur sound following the letter w

*When an /ur/ sound follows the letter **w** (but not **qu**) it is usually spelt **or** (e.g. word, worm, work, worship, worth). The important exception is were.*

Or sound before a l sound

*An /or/ sound before a /l/ sound is frequently spelt with the letter **a** (e.g. **all, ball, call, always**).*

Words ending in v

*English words do not end in the letter v unless they are abbreviations (e.g. rev.). If a word ends in a /v/ sound, **e** must be added after the **v** in the spelling (e.g. give, have, live, love, above). This may seem confusing because it suggests that the vowels should have their long sounds (as in alive, save and stove) but in fact there are very few words in the give/have category (i.e. words with short vowels) – they are mostly common words and are quickly learned. (There are, however, many multi-syllable adjectives which have an -ive ending, including addictive, abrasive, abusive, inactive and destructive.)*

Using -ant, -ent, -ance or -ence

*In deciding whether to use **-ant** or **-ent**, **-ance** or **-ence** at the end of a word, it is often helpful to consider whether there is a related word where the vowel sound is more clearly pronounced. When deciding, for example, between occupant or occupent, the related word occupation shows that the vowel letter must be **a**. Similarly, if unsure about residance or residence, the word residential shows that the letter must be **e**.*

(DCSF, 2010a: 105)

The problem of homophones, homographs and homonyms

A major source of humour in English-speaking countries centres on puns and plays on words, such as those in the following examples.

- I bet the butcher he couldn't reach the meat on the top shelf, but he refused to take the bet because the steaks were too high.

- I used to be a doctor but I lost patients.

- What happens to frogs who park on double yellow lines? They get toad away!

And the more modern:

- I changed my iPod name to Titanic – it's syncing now.

Puns are homophones – they are words which sound the same as other words but are spelled differently and have different meanings. They not only provide us with lots of opportunities for humour, but also lead to confusion and misconceptions in spelling. As well as homophones we also have homographs, which are words which are spelled in the same way but have different meanings and pronunciations, and homonyms, which have the same spellings but different pronunciations. Look at the examples below

Homophones (same sound but different spelling)	Homographs (same spelling but different pronunciation)	Homonyms (same spelling and pronunciation)
sea, see	bow (used to fire arrows), bow (bend from the waist)	down (in a lower position), down (feathers)
sew, so, sow	sow (seeds), sow (female pig)	
waste, waist	reading (books, etc.), Reading (town)	
their, there, they're	minute (60 seconds), minute (tiny)	
by, buy, bye	refuse (waste), refuse (decline)	
meet, meat	wind (moving air), wind (turn)	
patients, patience	wound (injury), wound (turned)	
principal, principle	desert (arid region), desert (to leave)	
male, mail		
lead (type of metal), led (took the lead)	lead (go first), lead (type of metal)	lead (go first), lead (dog's lead)
for, four, fore		

Dombey (2009) maintains that we construct patterns of expectation that prime us to recognise particular words and establish their meanings. For example, if we are scanning a train timetable, we see *Reading* as a place, not a process, and pronounce it accordingly. If we are writing about an accident, we will use the word *wound*, without thinking that it is also the past participle of the verb *to wind*.

Homophones present the biggest challenge for spelling. Some teachers teach their spellings in groups, focusing on the distinctions between the words, while others feel that this may confuse students and so teach words in 'families'. For example, rather than teach *where* and *wear,* and *there* and *their* together, they would teach *where* with *there* and *wear* with *tear* because they have similar spellings. *Their* is a common tricky word with few other words having the same vowel trigraph (eir), but it might be taught alongside *heir*.

Another approach could be to focus on wordplay and humour and to encourage children to look for examples of homophones in jokes and use dictionaries to find meanings where they are not immediately clear. There are many websites devoted to puns and plays on words.

Morphemes

You have already seen that we need to be able to read and spell far more words than we can ever actually be taught, so strategies are needed to help us when we encounter new words. Besides learning spelling generalisations, we can also focus on morphemes. Morphemes are the smallest units of meaning and can be prefixes, suffixes and root words. Look at the words below and identify the prefix, suffix and root word in each:

unlikely

distasteful

re-elected

You should have divided the words as follows:

un/like/ly

dis/taste/ful

re-/elect/ed

The prefixes are the morphemes placed at the beginning (*un-, dis-, re-*) to modify the root words in the middle (*like, taste, elect*), and the suffixes which go at the ends of words to modify them further (*-ly, -ful, -ed*). The root words are known as free morphemes, since they can stand alone as words, but the prefixes and suffixes are bound morphemes, since they need to be attached to words if they are to carry meaning. However, sometimes prefixes come to be used as words in their own right, especially in language used by young people, for example *dis-* is a prefix meaning *not* or *the opposite* (as in *disrespect*), but it has come to be used as a free morpheme and now appears in some dictionaries (*Don't diss me, man; Are you dissing me?*). Prefixes such as *mega-, super-* and *mini-* have also become words in their own right over time.

English, like many other languages, has thousands of words which include two or more morphemes, and these include compound words such as armchair, bookcase and doorknob, which are made up of two or more free morphemes. Try looking at a random page from a dictionary to see how many words are created from merging words together or adding prefixes and/or suffixes. On some pages you will find that every word begins with a prefix (try dis-, un-, re-, etc.), but look, too, at pages where the words do not begin with prefixes and you will find many examples of suffixes and compound words.

Research focus: Morphemes

Nunes and Bryant (2006) maintained that children found spelling difficult where words could not be predicted from the way they sound. They found that spelling difficulties can be reduced by drawing attention to the morphemes within words. Besides helping develop spelling, this approach also helped broaden children's vocabularies and enabled them to understand new words where the root was familiar. Nunes and Bryant concluded that it was important for teachers to:

- be aware of the role that morphemes play in spelling difficulties and of how they can be addressed;

- systematically teach about morphemes and their role in spelling;

- promote spelling and language development by teaching about morphemes.

British and American (US) English

Students are frequently exposed to text in American English in novels they study, song lyrics, computer games, on television, and in advertisements. In addition, many spellcheckers' default setting is American English. British and American spelling differs for several types of word. American English has gradually changed some spellings to more phonically regular versions, while British spelling has often retained the spellings of words from other languages in the form used in those languages. For example, for words ending with *-re* in British English, the American version often changes to *-er* as in *center* for *centre*, *theater* for *theatre* and *liter* for *litre*. All of these words originate from French which places the r before the e.

Why does this present a challenge?

If students regularly see versions of words with spellings which though correct in American English are not accepted in British English, they are likely to reproduce these spellings in their writing, possibly losing marks in exams or having job applications rejected as a result. However, given the plethora of American English texts available, it is important that they are aware of where the spelling patterns differ.

Differences between British and American spellings

The main areas of difference are as follows:

Words ending in -our
British English words ending in *-our* usually end in *-or* in American English, for example *colour – color*; *neighbour – neighbor*.

Words ending in a vowel plus l
In British English, the *l* is doubled in verbs ending in a vowel plus *l* when we add *-ed*, but the *l* is not doubled in American English. For example, *travelled – traveled*; *levelled – leveled*.

Words ending in -ize or -ise
In British English words which end with either *-ize* or *-ise* at the end are always spelled with *-ize* at the end in American English. For example, *organise* and *organize* are both acceptable in British English, but only *organize* is acceptable in American English.

Words ending in -yse
Verbs in British English that end in *-yse* are always spelled *-yze* in American English; for example, *paralyse – paralyze*.

Words spelled with double vowels
American English spells words which in British English are spelled with *oe* or *ae* just with an *e*, although both versions can sometimes be found in the USA. Examples include: *maneuver – manoeuvre*; *encyclopedia – encyclopaedia*.

Nouns ending with -ence
American English spells some nouns that end with *-ence* in British English with *-ense*. For example, *defense – defence*; *license – licence*.

Nouns ending with -ogue
American English uses either *-og* or *-ogue* for the endings of nouns which in British English end in *-ogue*. For example, *catalog – catalogue*; *dialog – dialogue*.

Besides exploring some of the British and American spelling differences, students might also look at some of the vocabulary differences between the two versions of English.

British	American
lorry	truck
trousers	pants
pavement	sidewalk
road	highway
glue	gum

(Continued)

(Continued)

British	American
trainers	sneakers
petrol	gas
café	diner
rubbish	trash

An exploration of vocabulary differences can be particularly valuable for English literature, where set books often originate from the USA, for example *To Kill a Mockingbird*, *Of Mice and Men* and *Holes*.

Invented spellings

Just to complicate spelling further, we are faced with invented spellings all around us when we go shopping or look at the music charts. These spellings tend to be phonically regular, but sometimes substitute a letter for a word (Toys R Us; U-Haul), or spell in a simplified way which would be unlikely to exist in a dictionary (Kwikfit), or involve puns (Beatles). It may be worth exploring some of these examples in conjunction with looking at some of the invented spellings students use in their day-to-day communications, for example, texting.

Does texting cause problems?

Finally in this section, it is worth looking at some of the research on the impact of texting on children's spelling. It might seem logical to argue that some of the invented spellings used by students when texting could have a detrimental effect upon their spelling. Indeed, Uthus (2007) argued that 'text-speak' is 'destroying the English language'. This view was supported by O'Connor (2009: 2) who believed that the deviant nature of 'text-speak' is causing the 'bastardization of language'. Lee (2002) maintained that students who frequently send text messages have been found to use bad grammar, punctuation and improper abbreviations in their academic writing.

However, there are strong counterclaims about the impact and indeed the value of texting. Crystal (2009: 172) argued that 'texting is one of the most innovative linguistic phenomena of modern times', which helps rather than hinders literacy. He states there is no evidence to suggest that children who use 'text-speak' cannot spell. Rather, he asserts, children must know how to spell words correctly before they are able to abbreviate them. This is because in order to substitute letters children must have an awareness of the original spelling. This is supported by Bloom (2010) who states that the use of 'text-speak' requires a sophisticated grasp of the English language. Moreover, Scanlon (2006) suggests that text messaging increases enthusiasm for reluctant writers, particularly those who experience difficulties with the transcriptional aspects of writing, such as spelling. She states that if children are to become committed writers then they must be motivated to write. She believes this can be successfully achieved through valuing text messaging as a legitimate form of writing in the literacy curriculum.

As with American English, a solution to any perceived problems may be to explore the vocabulary and spellings used, to ensure that students are aware of what is acceptable in different text types.

How to learn a spelling

You have now looked at some key challenges in learning to spell and at some solutions. Before looking at the next section, try Activity 4.4 below. It should alert you to the fact that we adopt different strategies for different words.

Activity 4.4

How do you know how to spell these words?

Wednesday

environment

separate

February

accommodation

ladies

monkeys

In this section you will meet the words in Activity 4.4 again and see examples of strategies which might be used to help us to spell them correctly.

Case study: A school spelling strategy applied for all students

A school in south-east England set up a working party of teachers, led by the Head of English, to devise a brief guide for spelling strategies which could be used by teachers in all subject areas. It was felt that if the guide was to be useful and easily accessible it should be presented as a single sheet of card with guidance on each side, and should be laminated. Each subject leader was to discuss the guide with colleagues and ensure that all understood the strategies provided and subscribed to its use. A similar, simplified guide was produced for students. It was agreed that it should be piloted in Years 7 and 8, reviewed, and then amended in the light of feedback from staff and students before being rolled out throughout the school. The guide is reproduced below.

→

LEARNING A SPELLING

Look-say-cover-write-check

This is the most basic strategy for learning to spell a word. The other strategies on this card are all linked to it. When faced with a new word to learn, look at the word carefully and at the sequence of letters; say the word aloud; cover it up; try to write it correctly; check to see if you were right. If you were, move on to another word; if you weren't, go through the process again.

Blending and segmenting

When saying a word you need to be sure that you are pronouncing it correctly. If in doubt, ask for help. When you say a word aloud segment it into its individual sounds (phonemes) and notice which letters (graphemes) represent each sound. For example, if learning to spell *parallel* you should segment it into /p/a/r/a/ll/e/l/. There are seven phonemes in parallel but eight letters. Notice that the /l/ sound in the middle is represented by two letters ll (a digraph) while the /l/ sound it the end is represented by a single l.

Identify and learn the 'tricky' bits

In the example above, you can see that for most people learning to spell parallel they will need to focus on the double l and the single l. These are the 'tricky' parts of the word. English words often have such 'tricky' bits and we can identify them when making our first attempts at writing the words. Look at the words below and identify the bits which might be tricky for some spellers:

separate

accommodate

pneumatic

Over-syllabification

Many people sound letters which are not usually sounded in some words to help them remember how to spell them. This is called over-syllabification. Look at the words below and consider how you might remember how to spell the tricky or silent bits:

Wednesday

February

raspberry

Over-syllabification in which we identify a 'tricky' part of a word which may not normally be sounded, such as in *Wednesday* and *February*, and then say the word with the sound included when we need to spell it (*Wed-nes-day, Feb-ru-ary*).

$\longrightarrow$

Syllables

For short words we can break them into individual sounds (phonemes) to help us to read and spell them. For longer words we might break them into syllables so that we can hear the sounds of each part of the word – *Oc-to-ber*.

Links between words

Learn words by analogy with others with similar spellings – could, would, should; bright, night, right, etc.

Morphemes

Find the base or root word within a word and learn the different morphemes (units of meaning) and their spellings – *lovely – love-ly; unlike – un-like.*

Compound words

Compound words are created when two words are combined to create a new word. For example, toothbrush, raincoat, football and pleasure-seeker. Try finding as many compound words as you can in a page of text and identify the words which come together to create them.

Mnemonics

Just as we make use of mnemonics as memory aids to remember the colours of the rainbow (Richard of York gave battle in vain – red, orange, yellow, green, blue, indigo, violet), points of the compass (never eat Shredded Wheat), we can create *mnemonics* to remember a tricky letter sequence in a word: could – can old ugly lions dance; because – big elephants can always understand small elephants, etc. This can be done for the tricky bits of words as well as for whole words. For example, *separate* is very often misspelled as 'seperate', but if you remember that sep<u>arat</u>e has a rat in it, you'll remember to use an a rather than an e in the middle.

Spelling rules and generalisations

Although there are many irregularities in English spelling, and some 'rules' have lots of exceptions, there are some generalisations which apply consistently. You could explore some of the following.

- Which letters are not used to end English words?
- What do you do to make a noun ending with 'y' plural?
- Which letter almost always follows 'q'?
- Do any English words begin with a double consonant?

The guidelines provided in 'Learning a Spelling' made teachers consider their own approaches to spelling and led some to use the strategies themselves to improve their own spelling, as well as to support their students as they learned subject-based terminology. A starting point was identified as helping to ensure that all Year 7 students could spell the names of the subjects on their timetables.

Activity 4.5   Spelling subject names

Look at the names of the subjects on the syllabus for Year 7 in one school:

Art and Design

Citizenship

Computing

Design and Technology

English

French

Geography

History

Mathematics

Music

Physical Education

Religious Education

How many of the names of the subjects above have irregular or tricky bits which students will need to learn in order to spell them correctly? Which of the strategies suggested in this chapter might you use to teach and learn the words? (See the Activities answers and discussion section at the end of the chapter for discussion.)

Supporting and developing spelling

In this chapter you have seen that spelling in English presents many challenges, particularly for children whose literacy skills are weak, but also for almost all students, given the complexities of the alphabetic code. However, you have also seen that there are many strategies available to help students to develop their spelling and to encourage them to look closely at words and their meanings. The goal in teaching spelling is to develop students' independence so that they have strategies available to them when they are unsure about how to spell a word. These strategies need not be complex and students will acquire them most effectively where there is a consistent approach to spelling across the curriculum. Reading and spelling should feature in every subject, and quite apart from the intrinsic importance of supporting students' literacy development, there is an increased emphasis upon accuracy in examinations in all subjects, which demands that every teacher should be a teacher of spelling.

Learning outcomes review

You should now have:

- an understanding of some of the challenges of teaching and learning English spellings;
- an appreciation of some strategies for teaching and learning spelling;
- an understanding of key aspects of spelling, including spelling rules and generalisations, morphemes, grapheme-phoneme correspondences and homophones and homographs;
- an awareness of some possibilities for studying spelling across the curriculum.

Self-assessment questions

1. What is a rime?
2. What is a morpheme and why is it important that students learn about morphemes?
3. Describe the process by which you can learn a spelling through *look, say, cover, write, check.*

Activities: answers and discussion

Activity 4.3   Developing spelling investigations

This activity could be developed into a focus on characters' names in stories and in history and religious education. Because spelling rules were not well established when many texts were written, there are variations in spellings. For example, William Shakespeare spelled his name in at least six different ways, including two different ways in his will, but he never spelled it as we now spell it: *Shakespeare*! For other subjects there will be opportunities to relate new vocabulary to words which students already know, to emphasise spelling generalisations. For example: in mathematics, quadrilateral and quad bike; in geography, population and popular.

Activity 4.5   Spelling subject names

The names of all of the subjects on the syllabus for Year 7 include 'tricky' bits, except Computing and, ironically, French, both of which are phonically regular. The "tricky" parts of the words are highlighted in bold type below:

Art and Design

Citizenship

Computing

Design and Technology

English

French

Geography

History

Mathematics

Music

Physical Education

Religious Education

For design, we might over-syllabify to help us remember the silent g, and similarly for mathematics we might sound the e, and for history emphasise the o, and for religious emphasise the i. All of these letters are often unsounded when we say the words. For citizenship we can relate the soft c to other words, particularly city, which is a root for the word. The /k/ sound at the end of music is not common and so needs to be focused upon, while the phys beginning for physical can be related to other words such as *physics*.

Further reading

For fascinating insights into the English spelling system and many other aspects of language:
Crystal, D. (2005) *How language works*. London: Penguin.

For discussion on texting and its impact on spelling:
Shortis, T. (2007) GR8 Txspectations: The creativity of text spelling. *English, Drama and Media*, June: 21–26 NATE.

References

Bloom, A. (2010) Texting aids literacy: Study confounds popular prejudice. *Times Educational Supplement*, 22 January, retrieved 4 June 2011 from: www.tes.co.uk/article.aspx?storycode=6033908

Cossu, G., Gugliotta, M. and Marshall, J. (1995) Acquisition of reading and written spelling in a transparent orthography: Two non parallel processes? *Reading and Writing: An Interdisciplinary Journal*, 7: 9–22.

Crystal, D. (2005) *How language works*. London: Penguin.

Crystal, D. (2009) *Txtng: The gr8 db8*. Oxford: Oxford University Press.

DCSF (2010a) National Strategies *Support for spelling*. 2nd edition. London: DCSF (accessed 1 January 2013) at: www.lancsngfl.ac.uk/nationalstrategy/literacy/download/file/Support_for_Spelling.pdf

DCSF (2010b) National Strategies Secondary 1 Key Leaflet *Teaching Struggling Readers*. London: DCSF.

DfE (2013) *The national curriculum in England framework document*. London: DfE.

DfES (2007) *Letters and sounds*. London: DfES.

Dombey, H. (2009) *Readings for discussion – the simple view of reading*. Available from: www.ite.org.uk/ite_readings/simple_view_reading.pdf (accessed February 2013).

Ehri, L. (2005) Learning to read words: Theory, findings, and issues. *Scientific Studies of Reading*, 9 (2): 167–88.

Frith, U. (1985) Developmental dyslexia, in Paterson, K. E., Marshall, J. C. and Coltheart, M. (eds) *Surface dyslexia*. Hover: Lawrence Erlbaum Associates.

Geva, E. and Siegel, L. S. (2000) Orthographic and cognitive factors in the concurrent development of basic reading skills in two languages. *Reading and Writing: An Interdisciplinary Journal*, 12: 1–30.

Goswami, U. (1995) Phonological development and reading by analogy: What is analogy, and what is it not? *Journal of Research in Reading*, 18 (2): 139–45.

Lee, J. (2002) I think, therefore IM, *The New York Times*, 19 September, retrieved 30 December 2013 from: http://query.nytimes.com/gst/fullpage.html?res=9F06E5D71230F93AA2575AC0A9649C8B63

Nunes, T. and Bryant, P. (2006) *Improving literacy through teaching morphemes*. London: Routledge.

O'Connor, A. (2009) *Instant messaging: Friend or foe of student writing?* Retrieved 30 December 2013 from: www.newhorizons.org/strategies/literacy/oconnor.htm

OECD (2010) *PISA 2009 at a glance*. OECD Publishing. Available from: http://dx.doi.org/10.1787/9789264095298-en (accessed 30 December 2013).

O'Sullivan, O. and Thomas, A. (2007) *Understanding spelling*. London: Routledge.

Parkinson, J. (2007) *i before e (except after c): Old-school ways to remember stuff*. London: Michael O'Mara Books Ltd.

Scanlon, J. (2006) Literacy for life: The world of signs and symbols, in Fisher, R. and Williams, M. (eds) *Unlocking literacy*. 2nd edition. London: David Fulton, pp. 205–18.

Spencer, K. (2002) English spelling and its contribution to illiteracy. *Literacy*, 36 (1) (April): 16–25.

Uthus, E. (2007) Text messages destroying our language. *The Daily of the University of Washington*, May 7. Retrieved 29 December 2013, from: http://dailyuw.com/news/2007/may/07/text-messages-destroying-our-language/

Venezky, R. L. (1973) Letter–sound generalizations of first, second, and third-grade Finnish children. *Journal of Educational Psychology*, 64: 288–92.

Waugh, D., Warner, C. and Waugh, R. (2013) *Teaching grammar, punctuation and spelling in primary schools*. London: Sage.

Wylie, R. E. and Durrell, D. D. (1970) Teaching vowels through phonograms. *Elementary English*, 47: 787–91.

5 The pedagogy of reading in Key Stage 3

Learning outcomes

By reading this chapter you will develop:

- an understanding of suitable teaching methods for developing students' ability to discriminate between sounds in engaging and interactive ways;
- an understanding of suitable teaching methods for developing students' higher-order reading skills;
- an awareness of some teacher-directed and independent activities which can be applied across the curriculum;
- some ideas for using varied sources for developing and extending students' reading skills.

2012 Teachers' Standards

2. Promote good progress and outcomes by pupils:

- demonstrate knowledge and understanding of how pupils learn and how this impacts on teaching.

3. Demonstrate good subject and curriculum knowledge:

- have a secure knowledge of the relevant subject(s) and curriculum areas, foster and maintain pupils' interest in the subject, and address misunderstandings;
- demonstrate an understanding of and take responsibility for promoting high standards of literacy, articulacy and the correct use of Standard English, whatever the teacher's specialist subject.

Introduction

So often, books on how to teach reading address the needs of early years or Key Stage 1 children. This chapter tackles how you can teach reading to Key Stage 3 students. These older students present different and very challenging problems from those of their younger counterparts. Their growing maturity and physical development, their social sensitivities, their uncertainties about themselves and their place in the world all conspire to make them a challenging group for the teacher who is helping them advance their reading.

Developing students' ability to discriminate between sounds

The basic pedagogic principle of systematic synthetic phonics (SSP) – that of matching sounds to graphemes in a systematic manner – potentially applies as much to teaching Key Stage 3 young people who are struggling with their reading as it does to teaching beginning readers. It is a useful tool with which to approach new vocabulary. Therefore it can also be a useful tool for Key Stage 3 students who are reasonably competent readers, but are challenged by new words. The important phrase in those last two sentences is 'a useful tool'. SSP is one of a number of strategies with which to attack new words. It might best be seen as a strategy of first resort.

Using systematic synthetic phonics with Key Stage 3

Below is an example of useful advice, adapted from the National Strategies' *Teaching Key Stage 3 Struggling Readers* (2010).

In primary school, students are taught phonic knowledge in a systematic way. This involves a four-stage process:

1. learning to blend CVC (consonant-vowel-consonant) words, for example 'b/i/g', 'ch/i/p';

2. recognising all 44 phonemes;

3. blending adjacent consonants (e.g. bl, br, dr, sp, tr);

4. knowing all long vowel phonemes.

Struggling readers in Key Stage 3 may benefit from going back over the same process as a way of embedding earlier learning that is insecure, or simply forgotten. You may find it useful to refer back to Chapters 1, 2 and 3, to provide yourself with a framework of systematic phonic information.

You can assess the phonic knowledge of Key Stage 3 students who are underperforming at reading (and spelling) against the four stages listed above. Once you have identified the students' strengths and weaknesses in phonics, then your teaching has to be based on moving them up through these stages.

Once these phonic skills are mastered, your students will still need ongoing help with their reading. It is important to remember that there is no hard-and-fast threshold in reading development, which, once reached, guarantees that the student will never need to resort to phonics-based reading strategies in the face of new words or phrases. Reading development is a continuum, arguably a lifelong one, and even the most competent, mature readers may encounter new and challenging phrases. This is the main justification for continuing to teach sound discrimination to struggling readers at Key Stage 3. It is an essential part of their survival kit.

Research focus

Henry (1997) points out that very poor readers may need help to improve their abilities to discriminate between different speech sounds. It may be that inability to distinguish between sounds is reducing their ability to decode, spell and

⟶

comprehend properly. If a student is able to read words slowly but has little under-standing of their meaning, this is likely to mean that he can decode, but do so slowly, with the result that his working memory is unable to piece together any flow of meaning (Maughan *et al.*, 2009). In other words, such students need to develop more speed, or fluency, to their reading because then the meanings of more words will still be accessible in the working memory. Comprehension can then increase. Researchers have found that in some students the causal links between vocabulary knowledge, decoding ability and comprehension can be considerable (Henderson *et al.*, 2011).

Evidence from research such as the above examples provides ideas for approaching the teaching of reading to Key Stage 3 students. It suggests that a focus on phonics is worthwhile, especially for the weakest readers, but that this is the first of a sequence of steps. Students then need to be moved on reasonably soon to concentrate on reading aloud with some pace. The primary school expression of asking students to read aloud 'with meaning' applies here. That is the next objective. The next step again might be to broaden vocabulary by increasing the student's word knowledge on a systematic basis. All these steps might need to precede a really struggling reader's development of improved comprehension.

Activity 5.1   Thinking about students who may be struggling with reading

1. If you teach a Key Stage 4 class, especially a lower set, the pressure of examination syllabuses may mean you have not had time in your teaching to consider whether reading *is* a challenge for any students. Take a few moments to reflect upon whether some might be struggling. What signs might you be looking for?

2. Do you ever ask students to read aloud? If you do, what happens?

3. If you don't ask them to read aloud, what might you need to be prepared for?

For some students with reading problems, a lack of a good range of vocabulary knowledge and word power is a major obstacle. The case study below shows how Mark overcame his problems with the new, challenging words and phrases when he arrived in Key Stage 3. On entry to Year 7 he had not been flagged as a struggling reader, but needed basic help nevertheless. The large number of new concepts and words and phrases across the curriculum was the source of his problems.

Case study: Overcoming reading challenges in Key Stage 3

At primary school Mark had found learning to read quite straightforward. Willing to please, he always practised his sounds and letters, and did his reading homework. Throughout Years 5 and 6 he was always seen as an accomplished reader, well able to cope with the school's reading curriculum.

But on reaching secondary school, Mark began to flounder. Having been confident and outgoing, his behaviour became more withdrawn. He was quieter, less cheerful, and 'harder to reach'. No one suspected a problem with reading until the start of the second term. During the Christmas holidays, Mark had become increasingly unhappy at the prospect of returning to school. Once the second term began, he failed to settle and started misbehaving. His form tutor, also his history teacher, quickly stepped in and spoke to all his subject teachers, and discovered his performance was heading into a tailspin. She met Mark's parents, who told her how conscientious he had been with reading homework at primary school. That rang alarm bells – reading as a task in itself was not set in any subjects for homework. Instead, homework meant under-standing and applying new terms and concepts.

Mark's tutor realised that maybe Mark's primary school success might have been because much of the homework and schoolwork had been aligned to the primary goal of acquiring, developing and extending reading. Now, at secondary school, pressures to learn came from many sources. Being able to read to a level sufficient for the Key Stage 3 curriculum was a vital skill that a boy as bright as Mark was assumed to possess.

His form tutor asked all Mark's teachers to produce a list of the top 20 important new words and concepts in their subjects. These became a starting point for Mark's recovery, both of his reading and his self-esteem. He learned these, as extra homework, over four weeks. Then, after half term, he moved on to creating his own subject dictionaries of key words and phrases, and their meanings, in each subject.

By the start of term three, Mark was far more confident as a learner and made steady progress throughout Key Stage 3 in every subject.

Discussion

Mark had been at risk of being classed as a poor reader in Year 7. If that had happened, he might have been placed in low-ability groups. Very possibly he would have found his lessons unchallenging. One can imagine that Mark might have become unhappy and ceased to find school engaging. The steps taken by his form tutor were very important in averting that kind of development.

Some teachers might find it hard to decide what to use as teaching materials for older struggling readers. Clearly, most if not all such students are unlikely to respond to the same teaching materials as their early years counterparts. Indeed the considerate teacher would not start there. A three-step process is helpful with learners of all ages, especially those who have reached Key Stage 3 and still find reading a difficult and daunting skill. The three steps for selecting suitable teaching materials are shown in Table 5.1 below.

Table 5.1   The three steps for selecting suitable teaching materials

Step 1	Identify the problematic aspects of reading (this needs analysis).
Step 2	Match suitable teaching methods to the identified aspects of need.
Step 3	Match suitable teaching resources to the identified teaching methods.

Each step will now be considered in turn.

Step 1: Identify problematic aspects of reading

A simple and reasonably quick and efficient alternative method for identifying a student's reading problems is to spend a short time on two ways into the student's internal reading mechanism – sight and sound.

First, listen to the student reading a word list containing words that he/she typically struggles with, and note errors on a parallel list. This can be done by you, or by a classroom assistant or other learning support professional. The goal here is to identify the student's common reading errors. For example, is a particular sound–symbol relationship, such as the pair of graphemes 'pr' as in 'preach', being recognised in words where it is the initial phoneme, but not when it appears in other positions (such as medial or final) in such words as 'approve'? If so, the problem lies more in the student needing to recognise the same sound–symbol relationship in new or less frequent words rather than in teaching the actual relationship as if from new. Another possible problem may be that certain sound–symbol relationships are never recognised. If this is the case, then those need to be learned as basic essential phonic knowledge.

Second, ask the student to listen to a recording of a short set of random, simple words and repeat them. You are not asking the student to read, and he should concentrate on listening. Note which words the student stumbles over or has difficulty pronouncing. You are looking for signs of any sounds the student cannot hear. This is looking into their auditory perception.

Third, ask the student to listen to a recording of another set of simple words and simultaneously find the print version from a list or set of words. Don't make the words heard and seen too demanding or numerous. Every time the student hears a word that he thinks matches a printed one, he has to select the word. The idea here is to identify any sounds that the student has difficulty relating to their print counterpart.

If you wish to look more deeply into identifying reading problems, then you might like to consider doing what are called 'running records'. There are some suggestions for ways into this in the further reading section towards the end of this chapter.

Taken together and examined carefully, the results of investigating both the visual and auditory aspects of the internal reading mechanism may enable you to identify some errors that the student is making always and some which he/she is making sometimes. You'll be able to see which of these are made when attempting to read by looking at words on the page; which errors the student is making in hearing sounds on their own; and which errors the student is making when matching words from sound to sight. While you may not reach a complete picture of the student's reading problems, you can at least begin to set out some of the problem issues, as shown in Table 5.2.

Table 5.2   Identifying a student's reading problems

List of suspected problem words	Errors reading (from sight)	Errors repeating spoken words	Errors matching sound to print

Step 2: Match suitable teaching methods to the identified needs

The key word with respect to matching teaching methods to needs is 'suitable', because the selection of appropriate teaching methods is vital. However, it is also something that teachers' planning all too often ignores. As teachers we tend to place great trust in what we know our students will respond to doing, or what last year's equivalent group enjoyed. Or we rush to lay our hands on teaching materials (resources) before asking ourselves if they are fit for purpose. A report on research into the teaching methods used to teach SEN students (DfE, 2004) found that in some classrooms teaching methods were not differentiated, and in many classrooms teaching methods were not differentiated sufficiently to meet all students' needs. The report recommends that while inclusive teaching of SEN students is generally welcome, a key to successful teaching of such students, indeed all students, is to employ a variety of teaching methods in teaching a class with students of varying abilities. It is worth thinking through what teaching methods might be applicable for the student(s) in question. A frequently heard but still powerful point is that *if* a true SSP approach has been tried before, maybe repeatedly, and has apparently failed, then different teaching methods should be attempted. The counter to that is that any number of contextual reasons external to the student might be causing poor learning of phonics. These could include distracting elements in the class, or the teaching might not have been very clear and structured. So the message is to be open-minded about possible reasons for reading problems, and do what you can to identify suitable teaching methods.

Working through the process of identifying problem areas summarised in Table 5.1 should help point you in the right direction for matching teaching methods to needs. You will know whether problems predominate in one direction or both. This will give you a handle on how to approach your teaching. If the student cannot securely repeat aloud sounds that are only heard, then work needs to be done on teaching clear sound perception. In some cases this may call for specialist help, although such cases will more usually have been picked up and worked on with younger children. With a student who has no problem recognising sounds and repeating them accurately, your focus needs to be on improving the student's print recognition of those familiar sounds. If the student cannot securely match sound to print, then you should find focusing on sound–print matching work is beneficial.

Step 3: Match suitable teaching materials to the teaching methods

Now you have to be guided both by whatever your analysis of reading needs has led you to identify *and* by the teaching methods you have selected, and find suitable teaching materials. The process is summarised below in Table 5.3.

Table 5.3   *The three steps for matching teaching materials to teaching method*

Step 1	List the problems you have identified, prioritising the most prevalent sound-symbol relationships and noting their directionality.
Step 2	Enter which teaching methods you have selected as possibly suiting which problems. Avoid being attracted to methods that do not relate to the needs you have identified.
Step 3	Construct or search for teaching materials that use these methods and are simple, stimulating and relevant.

Teaching materials don't have to be elaborate. To start you off, try compiling your own bank of some simple word and picture sets. This might take time, but is an invaluable resource that you can expand as opportunity arises and that you can take with you to any school. Indeed, rather than make these sets yourself, try getting the students to collect pictures and illustrations of words containing the sounds. If you need these sets for younger students, then KS3 students might be all the more prepared to create them.

Finally, have a look through the next two sections for some other teaching activities and materials you might like to try.

Teacher-directed and independent activities which can be applied across the curriculum
Teacher-directed activities across the curriculum

From an inadequate reader's viewpoint, the fact that there is a range of subjects and teachers in secondary school is a potential source of risk and uncertainty when it comes to reading. Experiences will differ, but teacher responses to inadequate reading may vary widely. Some may be very experienced in supporting such readers, others simply may not, and others again, however experienced, may not know of possible solutions. The inadequate reader may experience such differing levels of challenge across subjects that even if teachers across two or three subjects utilise similar learning activities, then some consistency will very likely assist their improvement in reading and, very probably, be beneficial to their learning in those subjects.

Teacher-directed activities consist of more than the teacher telling students what to do: they involve the teacher taking the critical decisions about learning, such as how the task is to be tackled, by whom, for how long, and whether it is completed acceptably. Control over what is learned is exercised by the teacher. For this reason, if for no other, it may be hard to get agreement with colleagues in other curricular areas to run extensive teacher-directed activities along similar lines to each other. It is probably more feasible to agree to run in common some specific activities that use a short amount of time, are focused and enjoyable. Five-minute lesson starters, which focus each week on a different aspect of language across the subjects, can work well. For example, week one might involve each subject's teacher listing ten technical terms new to that subject; week two might move on to five new concepts; week three might focus on associating the new technical terms with specific examples of their existence. Each week's activity should be mainly or wholly oral, led by the teacher, rehearsed by the students, with board work as a supporting medium.

Independent activities across the curriculum

A major characteristic of independent activities is that much (but not all) control over learning moves from the teacher to the students. Projects, topic work and thematic work are all examples of the style of independent activity that can be run across the curriculum. The key to making these successful in developing and extending students' reading is for a small group of like-minded subject teachers to devise and agree some guidelines for a cross-curricular piece of work. The value of cross-curricular working, when successfully implemented, is immense; students' levels of interest and motivation to learn can rise steeply; they accomplish more; take more pride in their work; make links across subjects in a number of ways (such as transfer of factual knowledge, higher-order skills); and develop good learning habits.

Research focus

Teaching a class full of independent learners may sound very appealing. In fact, there is little agreement as to what an independent learner is, and how to create one. A review of research into independent learning (DCSF, 2008) found that many different terms are used that have similar meanings ('self-regulated' learning is one). It also found agreement in the literature that independent learning meant far more than students working on their own. In fact, the role of the teacher was as essential as, but different from, that in a whole-class form of teaching. Teachers need to teach and promote 'learning how to learn'.

Discussion

Learning how to learn might well sound rather glib: the sort of expression that trips smoothly off the tongue. It is a patterned behaviour and means students actually being aware of what they do when they learn. It often means drawing attention to learning as it is happening, to remind students of the progress they have made and the behaviour that has helped them get there. The goal is that they become 'mindful' learners. This would entail such behaviours as giving their full attention, focusing on the task, identifying the learning objective before they commence and bearing it in mind through the learning episode.

As a practitioner, you will already be aware that such things are more easily said than done. There isn't such a big step, however, between 'learning' and 'learning how to learn'. Activity 5.2 tries to lead you to think of what 'learning how to learn' might mean in reality.

Activity 5.2 Thinking about moving on from learning to learning how to learn

1. How do you usually check your students have learned something?

2. What steps might you take to encourage them to look at themselves learning?

3. How might you turn that into regular classroom routines?

An aspect of reading that many teachers are keen to see their students acquire is higher-order reading skills. Once the ability to decode at a basic level and read aloud with some smoothness has been achieved, comprehension becomes a key skill for teachers to see established in all their students. In fact, there are several higher-order reading skills, and often they are summed up into the one word, or concept, 'comprehension'. Examples of skills that are subsumed by the term 'comprehension' might include the skills of analysis, synthesis, inference and deduction. Encouraging the development of higher-order skills can be a very satisfying aspect of teaching and learning, as the following case study shows.

Case study: Higher-order reading skills – a cross-curricular success story

Misha and Jo taught English and geography respectively at an urban comprehensive. They joined forces to run a joint cross-curricular project to run during the first half of the autumn term, culminating in a week of group presentations, rated by the students themselves. A mid-ability Year 9 class was selected, and students had to

→

work in small groups of between three and five. The aim was to get students using higher-order reading skills in analysing, interpreting, selecting and synthesising information from a variety of sources. The twofold goal was for each group to prepare and produce a presentation on food supply problems in an underdeveloped part of the world and to produce a list of basics for a solution.

The teachers agreed in advance a set of ground rules for the students: high expectation of quality work; insistence on excellent behaviour and contribution from each individual; allocation of pre-set roles. Misha and Jo also agreed their own ground rules: clear objectives on each subject's contribution in terms of content and role – geography took the lead role in focussing each group's topic, identifying and interpreting the evidence; English led on composing, creating and giving a public presentation. They also fronted the project with a week of explicit teaching on the higher-order reading skills they wanted the students to develop. Finally, they also agreed a weekly catch-up and planning session.

The project was successful on many levels – hoped-for and unexpected. Students enjoyed it, learned a lot, and worked collaboratively – albeit with a few teething problems from one or two individuals who had to have a short 'time out' in order to learn to share or participate. Unexpected gains were the development in students of more mature and positive attitudes to learning; sustained motivation to learn in each subject was noticeable well beyond the period of the project. Two years later, students still fondly recall their first 'grown-up' project. Another unlooked for side effect was that Misha and Jo themselves both enjoyed the work immensely. They found themselves learning more about each other's subjects and their role in the curriculum. The higher-order reading skills benefited other subjects as well.

Discussion

Don't be daunted by the idea of taking on the promotion of higher-order reading skills among your students. The message from this case study is that, provided students can explore ideas and be creative along the way, you will achieve your objective.

Using varied resources

Trying to match resources to needs can be demanding. Finding resources that are reasonably attractive and user-friendly and also ensure progression, can be an even bigger challenge. Teachers' lives are too busy to spend much time weighing up the pros and cons of a whole range of materials. Try looking at a range of online sources for ideas – teachers' blogs, archived Teachers TV and archived Literacy Strategy materials. Twitter groups among teachers are increasingly popular for sharing resources and are a growing source of continuous professional development. It is obviously important to observe all the relevant professional protocols when using online media, and providing you do this, then you can discover a wealth of new ideas and materials. Sharing ideas is a big time-saver because someone else has already road-tested them for you.

As a general rule, UK teachers should look at US educational resource websites with some caution. US state and federal education systems and school structures are so very different from UK ones that care is needed in assessing the transferability of teaching ideas. Good-quality teaching approaches, wherever they originate, need to fit closely with your requirements. Follow the thinking set out in Table 5.3 and avoid grabbing at resources that in the end only provide 'busy work'.

Matching maturity levels and literacy needs

Try to ensure you tap into age-appropriate materials as well as teaching methods. Young people are quick to sense if they are being spoken down to. Nothing will be more off-putting to students in early adolescence than something that makes them feel they are being taught in the same ways and with the same materials as they were in primary school. That doesn't mean you have to go for super-sophisticated techniques. Often the very simplest are best. The key is to select materials and methods that are pitched at or very slightly above their maturity levels.

The idea of 'captains, experts or leaders' is a good way to encourage independent learning and at the same time appeals to Key Stage 3 students. It has the added benefits of promoting many higher-order skills, such as finding and evaluating information, collaborating, listening to others and so on. In the case study below you will see how Max discovered this when he tried it out at his middle school.

Case study: Developing independent learners via captains, experts and leaders

Max is a teacher in a middle school in Northumberland. He is keen to develop leadership skills in his Year 8 English classes to encourage higher-order thinking skills and resilience. Over the year he has been working with his colleagues at the secondary school that the students will be moving on to in Year 9. Their joint focus has been on the increased independent learning the students will face as they move into the secondary phase. To this end Max has planned many of his lessons with resilience and independence as the main focus. He has created team exercises in most of his lessons where a nominated expert, captain or leader is used to drive the lesson aims forward and to act as a point of peer reference before the students come to the teacher. These leaders are often chosen on ability, but also to encourage confidence building and enthusiasm, as he recognises that it is not just knowledge that makes a good leader. Initially he had expected the students to resent other members of the class being made a leader but was surprised to find that they not only liked it but were more open and talkative to a peer expert than he generally found they were with him.

The nominated students are primed before the lesson with the knowledge they will need and the planned lesson discussed. Their role is made clear and this avoids any confusion when tasks are being explained to the class. They are given a series of questions that they can use to encourage higher-order thinking from their group, for example: 'Can you give me another word that would describe that process?'; 'But what is behind the author's intentions? What is the subtext?' An additional advantage of this insight into higher-order questioning is that the leaders themselves have to think in this way to elicit such responses from the students, who are now responding to them as the 'captain' of their 'team'.

For example, when working on a section of *Romeo and Juliet* to perform in front of the class, each group is given a nominated 'director'. This student may or may not take part in the presentation themselves but will certainly co-ordinate, cast and direct it and work with the teacher on what the scene needs to show to aid the whole class's understanding of difficult parts of the text. They are given the text extract to read through so they are confident about the language delivery needed and are told what emphasis the teacher wants them to make clear in the meaning of the text. After that it is up to the leaders as to how the performance unfolds!

Max ensures that leaders and experts are changed regularly but he also makes it clear that there are certain skills and attributes that he is looking for in his experts. This not only outlines the criteria for good leadership but also encourages others in the group to develop these skills, so that they too can lead in their turn. The students have responded well and now fully expect to turn to each other for solutions, not just the teacher. They are proud to be leaders and it is desirable to become one. Their independence has reached a level where they often assume the mantle of the expert without being asked in other informal group work.

Discussion

Giving students responsibility is a highly effective way to engage their interest and motivation to learn. Using leaders and experts or similar techniques is a good example because the the importance of the roles is so evident to everyone in the class. Unless you have a very reticent student, they will all be very eager to take on the roles.

Lessons cannot always be, or be allowed to be, as entertaining as those involving leaders and experts, despite the fact that excellent work came out of the example in the case study. Often, teachers need to focus hard on making sure those students for whom reading is demanding are using phonic skills in reading and writing.

Applying phonics in meaningful reading and writing activities

In Chapter 1, you were introduced to the Simple View of Reading. It would be helpful to look back and remind yourself of the SVR while reading this next section. One of the SVR's most helpful features is that it links language comprehension with word recognition. For Key Stage 3 teachers, successful language comprehension is essential in competent reading. Often, in the busy mainstream classroom, students for whom comprehension is a real challenge may not be picked up, or they may be seen as having general language difficulties, and may be set word recognition exercises. Such work may not be very helpful. Better would be a clear assessment based on SVR principles that reveals their strengths and weaknesses in a systematic way.

A quick and easy way into assessing students' comprehension diagnostically is to use small groups for one-to-one talk and questioning. Go for questions that probe how much the student has comprehended from their reading of a text. This entails exploring their level of thinking. There are three levels of your students' thinking that, as a Key Stage 3 teacher, you are expecting to see.

1. *Literal understanding*: can the student recall information that is directly stated in the text?

2. *Deductive and inferential thinking*: deductive thinking is where students work out answers from information contained in the text; they have to deduce the answer from facts in the text. Inferential reasoning is where students bring their own knowledge to help in making sense of the text and answering questions. They infer, i.e. they use logic and reasoning and information from the text, but in comparison with deduction there is more of a sense of going beyond precisely what is in the text.

3. *Evaluating and responding to text*: here students go beyond the text and make a reasoned judgement or response to the text. They might compare it in certain respects with other texts.

Clearly, these three levels are progressive, and you are looking to move your students from the literal and on to the deductive, inferential and evaluative levels.

Case study: Two Key Stage 3 students with difficulties in reading comprehension

Student A

Satish was a Year 9 student who had good word recognition but weak comprehension skills. He could read aloud a page from any subject's text, and appear not to stumble. In fact, he read very quickly. However, he didn't make use of intonation, and sounded rather 'robotic'. When she asked Satish questions about what he had just read, his geography teacher, Janet, noticed he had in fact understood very little. Janet decided a sound- and print-rich language environment was essential for Satish. She spoke to three other teachers, of English, history and biology, who all agreed to join her in a six-week project based on Satish's and three other students' very similar needs.

They agreed that the basic principle of the project would be to set aside some time each week of the project for the small group to hear texts read fluently and with good intonation by the teaching assistant, while they simultaneously followed the print version. The TA would then take the group step by step through the text, asking questions for literal understanding and explaining any obstacle to factual understanding.

For the first two weeks, the teacher of each subject set aside some time for listening comprehension activities. Each teacher used an extract of text that had been recorded in sound (CD, web-based) and students took it in turns to listen and stop the recording twice to devise questions to ask the other students. Students took turns asking their questions of each other and rated the answers according to how informed they were.

For weeks three and four, the TA ensured that, following the reading during group time, she asked students questions that required deductive, inferential and evaluative responses. Homework was set to reinforce their learning by requiring written answers to questions at these same levels.

In the final two weeks of the project, Janet and her three colleagues focussed on rein- tegrating the small group into their mainstream classes. Bridging activities were used with the whole class, based on the three levels of thinking with which Satish and his group were now becoming familiar. Extra support by way of laminated prompt lists of each subject's key words and their meanings helped them progress.

Student B

Nina was a Year 7 student with weak reading comprehension and poor word recognition. She arrived in Year 7 with her reading assessed as just inside National Curriculum Level 3. Her phonic knowledge was muddled and she had low motivation to read. Her attitude towards school was becoming disaffected and she was developing low self-esteem.

In a term of special needs support, a learning programme was devised for Nina which took her through a staged sequence of learning and revision. First, Nina was taken back to first principles in understanding written language. She was taught again how to write each letter of the alphabet, and as she learned how to form them she was taught the sound they made. This was the basic building block for developing her word recognition skills.

Second, Nina was given a starter set of 50 common words (can, come, could, was, they, some, while, etc.) which she had to learn *by sight*. It was important that she learned to recognise them instantly. This equipped her with a basic word bank which was slowly but steadily added to and which began to give Nina a sense of achievement. Little by little, her disaffection lessened and her self-esteem grew.

Third, Nina's decoding ability was developed. Using the SSP approach outlined earlier in this book (especially Chapter 4) Nina was retaught sound–symbol relationships in a sequence of stages, which grew progressively more challenging.

After ten weeks, Nina returned to the mainstream classroom on a gradual basis. By the end of term she was reintegrated and was making steady progress in her reading comprehension.

Discussion

The examples of Satish and Nina illustrate the necessity of taking students back to early stages of reading skill development in order to start rebuilding both their skills and their confidence as readers. Sometimes, the source of the problem lies way back in the past: possibly an interrupted phase in their primary education through illness, or perhaps even because of inadequate teaching. As secondary teachers we must be aware that some of our students have experienced problems, delays and upsets in their process of becoming readers and may have missed out on a vital step. They need a focussed and effective intervention of reading support.

Suggested activities relevant to students' interests

It's often surprising how creative teachers are without even realising their talents. An idea that started as a small-scale attempt to encourage students to consider literacy in different cultures soon evolved into an absorbing cross-curricular project, as staff at Castlemere School (not its real name) discovered.

Case study: Cross-curricular links with cultural literacy

A secondary school with a strong reputation for the performing arts, Castlemere has broadened its definition of literacy to include the notion of 'cultural literacy' as a desirable outcome for its students and staff. Initially this was to introduce students to a wider variety of plays, books, music and art. The initiative began with regular theatre visits to see dance and extraordinary (rather than immediately popular) theatre. Students began to see the arts as more challenging than simply a yearly pantomime and a reality television show. Workshops were encouraged and staff and students enjoyed masterclasses from actors and worked with innovative Theatre in Education companies.

This began to have an impact on student expectation and the curriculum. English and arts staff found they had a ready arsenal of reference points where students had experienced, watched and heard art and media that had surprised and challenged them. These occasional trips and experiences became a logical but essential part of the experience of the students in the school. The school acknowledged the impact that this had on students' readiness to learn. Their growing eagerness to take on more challenging reading in English and conceptual writing and devising in drama and media was noted. Wanting to build on this and also find a more cost-effective way to introduce students to excellent, challenging and intelligent fare, the school subscribed to the web-based sharing site Digital Theatre Plus: digitaltheatreplus.com

→

They found that the site had well-filmed examples of plays, interviews, workshops and teachers' notes on a variety of recent popular plays and performances. These ranged from renowned modern Shakespeare texts (*Much Ado About Nothing* with David Tennant and Catherine Tate) to cutting-edge contemporary theatre (*Lovesong* by Abi Morgan and Frantic Assembly). For a modest sum, affordable on a school budget, both staff and students had access to excellent examples of theatre that often backed up the challenging reading on the curriculum.

Having access to this changed the work that is done in class and formed a large part of teacher planning and schemes of work. Current schemes were changed to suit what was available and the range of expertise grew for both students and staff. Evenings were set aside where staff and students were invited in for 'an evening at the theatre' – not unlike National Theatre screenings in local cinemas. Students had free access to world-class theatre. They now expect to be stretched when watching and reading plays. Seeing them performed exceptionally well enhances their understanding and contributes to their real and cultural literacy.

Discussion

The key to Castlemere's success was the way they moved students along a widening path of cultural literacy experiences. They started with introducing students to experiences that were close to, but not quite within, their normal range. Then Castlemere brought in experiences that steadily expanded students' cultural horizons by gradually introducing them to wider and more experimental experiences.

Finally, it is also possible to work differently and start where the students are, within their comfort zones, and work outwards from those. Here are some ideas that teachers of young people who struggle with reading have found helpful in other secondary schools.

- Use reading partners – you can match stronger with weaker readers or pair readers of very similar ability. Both ways have advantages, but watch out for the disadvantage that a stronger reader might lose interest if paired with a very much weaker reader. Reading partners are also useful for far more than simply 'reading'. Use them as the basis for any number of comprehension activities and tasks, such as question setting and answering, finding out specialist information, making evaluations about a text and using evidence from the text to support those evaluations.

- Set class spelling competitions based on words and sentences – a weekly competition in which each student has to find five (or more, you decide) new words and their meanings specific to a subject. You can gradually increase the number and/or level of challenge.

- Use mind maps or spidergrams (look these up on Google) to map out in advance the essential content of a text. Present this to weaker readers and explain that it is a diagram representing the information in the text that the class is about to study. Over time, students can move on to developing their own spidergrams based on text they have read. This helps consolidate their understanding and gets them used to various alternatives to text as ways of representing information.

This chapter has covered a very large topic – how to teach reading to struggling older readers. The breadth of this topic may mean that some parts strike you as more immediately relevant or helpful than others. You may find you need to consult or return to some sections and not others. The two underlying themes of the chapter have been to give you some understanding of good practice regarding teaching these students, and to generate ideas for teaching from which you can extend your own teaching repertoire.

Learning outcomes review

You should now have:

- an understanding of suitable teaching methods for developing students' ability to discriminate between sounds in engaging and interactive ways;
- an understanding of suitable teaching methods for developing students' higher-order reading skills;
- an awareness of some teacher-directed and independent activities which can be applied across the curriculum;
- some ideas for using varied sources for developing and extending students' reading skills.

Self-assessment questions

1. How might you develop better comprehension skills in all pupils in a class?
2. What new ideas can you see yourself using in your lessons to help support students with reading difficulties?

Activities: answers and discussion

Activity 5.1   Thinking about students who may be struggling with reading

1. My bottom set Year 10 class don't engage very much in my science lessons. They are often bored. I think I talk at them a lot and then present them with worksheets. That's when they start talking too much. Some students, now I think of it, really depend on others to help them read the worksheets.

2. I rarely ask anyone to read aloud. If I do, it's for one of two reasons: first, I want a change of 'voice' so that my voice isn't all the students hear. If that's the reason then I always ask a student who I know can read sufficiently well. The other reason I might ask someone to read is to quell a minor disturbance, so it's a bit of a threat, or 'stick'.

3. I suppose they might clam up, or go so slowly it's uncomfortable for everyone else to listen to.

Activity 5.2   Thinking about moving on from learning to learning how to learn

1. I set a short test or writing task. Or I might ask some questions at the end of the lesson or unit of study.

2. I might ask them to talk to a partner about how that sequence of learning felt. They might keep a short journal about each week's learning. I'd have to be careful they kept the focus on how they learned.

3. I might have some pre-set questions on the whiteboard which I get them to answer after each unit. Such as, 'How I kept my attention on what I was learning'; 'How I know if I've understood the learning objective'; 'How I know if I've managed to learn something'. I could remind them about these questions during the working sessions. Once these become regular parts of the wrap-up for each unit of work, I could occasionally have short class discussions about learning to learn.

Further reading

This chapter has explained some basic ideas for noting struggling readers' reading mistakes. You might have heard of a system for identifying reading problems for younger students called running records of reading. This is based on what is called 'miscue analysis', where 'cues' are signals the reader uses to select a reading strategy. An early pioneer of this system was Marie Clay (1993) and a pdf version of her publication *Running Records for Classroom Teachers* may be found at: http://sbagley.webs.com/Running%20Records%20-%20Marie%20M.%20Clayassessment2.pdf

A reasonably simple self-tutoring guide has been written for the teacher who wishes to use running records systematically (Johnstone, 2000) Running records are handy for checking a student's progress, comparing groups of students and for matching students to texts with sufficient challenge.

To make a running record, the teacher or assistant marks a student's reading errors on a copy of the text as it is read aloud by the student. Examining the pattern of errors helps identify the most frequent. Clay's publication explains how to pick up errors, and how to code them. It explains how to categorise and interpret the information.

References

Bonifacci, P. and Snowling, M. J. (2008) Speed of processing and reading disability: A cross-linguistic investigation of dyslexia and borderline intellectual functioning. *Cognition,* 107 (3): 999–1017.

Clay, M. M. (1993) *An observational survey of early literacy achievement.* Auckland: Heinemann.

Department for Children, Skills and Families (DCSF) (2008) Research Report 051, *Independent learning literature review.* London: HMSO.

Department for Education (DfE) (2004) Research Report 516, *Teaching strategies and approaches for students with special educational needs: A scoping study*. Davis, P. and Florian, L., Manchester University. London: HMSO.

Henderson, L.-M., Baseler, H., Clarke, P., Watson, S. and Snowling, M. (2011) The N400 effect in children: Relationships with comprehension, vocabulary and decoding. *Brain and Language*, 117 (2): 88–99.

Henry, M. (1997) The decoding/spelling continuum: Integrated decoding and spelling instruction from pre-school to early secondary school. *Dyslexia*, 3: 178–89.

Johnstone, P. J. (2000) *Running records: A self-tutoring guide*. York, Maine: Stenhouse Press.

Maughan, B., Messer, J., Collishaw, S., Pickles, A., Snowling, M., Yule, W. and Rutter, M. (2009) Persistence of literacy problems: Spelling in adolescence and at mid-life. *Journal of child psychology and psychiatry*, 50 (8): 893–901.

6 Tracking, assessing and intervening in students' learning

Learning outcomes

By reading this chapter you will develop:

- knowledge of methods for monitoring students' progress and diagnostic assessment;
- awareness of possible deficits in Key Stages 3 and 4 students' learning and how these might be addressed;
- familiarity with a range of intervention programmes and resources;
- some strategies for working with colleagues to develop a whole-school approach across curricular areas.

2012 Teachers' Standards

3. Promote good progress and outcomes by pupils:

- be accountable for pupils' attainment, progress and outcomes;
- be aware of pupils' capabilities and their prior knowledge, and plan teaching to build on these;
- guide pupils to reflect on the progress they have made and their emerging needs;
- demonstrate knowledge and understanding of how pupils learn and how this impacts on teaching.

6. Make accurate and productive use of assessment:

- know and understand how to assess the relevant subject and curriculum areas, including statutory assessment requirements;
- make use of formative and summative assessment to secure pupils' progress;
- use relevant data to monitor progress, set targets, and plan subsequent lessons;
- give pupils regular feedback, both orally and through accurate marking, and encourage pupils to respond to the feedback.

Introduction

Secondary school teachers now work to a high degree of accountability compared with previous generations of teachers in the UK. The main source of this accountability is the very public pressure of school league tables. So much now depends upon a school's National Curriculum assessment and public examinations performance year by year. One consequence is that many educational ideas that were popular in the 1990s and early 2000s, such as the school effectiveness movement, have been superseded by far more specific, detailed and tailored approaches for improving student learning. These aim at targeting precisely where teachers might focus their teaching, and how they assess their effectiveness. This chapter aims to help you understand and use some of these ideas in order to raise student learning through improving their reading effectiveness.

Methods for monitoring students' progress and diagnostic assessment

If your training year gave you some basic information and experience about monitoring students' progress and using diagnostic assessment to inform your planning for their learning, then you already have some potentially very useful knowledge. You may recall from your training that much research evidence points to why we should undertake monitoring and assessment for reading.

Research focus: Why monitor and assess for reading in the secondary school?

Teachers' daily lives at school are full of procedures and routines they have to follow. Sometimes, we can lose sight of *why* they are important. So why do we monitor and assess? Here are summaries of reasons why two groups of researchers in the United States believe monitoring and assessing reading in the secondary school are important.

- Monitoring student progress helps teachers use student performance data to continually evaluate the effectiveness of their teaching and make more informed teaching decisions. This applies as much to reading in the secondary school as it does in the primary school, in students who have low reading levels (Safer and Fleischman, 2005).

- When teachers use systematic monitoring to track their students' progress in reading . . . they are better able to identify students in need of additional or different forms of instruction, they design stronger teaching programmes, and their students achieve better (Fuchs and Fuchs, 1999).

While much of the research evidence from the USA may not readily transfer to another national context, these points about the value of monitoring and assessment are sufficiently general to relate to the UK.

There are further reasons that explain why monitoring and assessing reading skills are important in the secondary school. Subject staff are understandably very focussed on whether their students can use and apply information gleaned from reading texts. This takes us into an area about which there is little research – subject applications, or uses, of reading skills.

Activity 6.1   Thinking about why we monitor and assess progress

Take a quick look at your school and departmental policies on monitoring and assessment. As you do so, think about the two points in the above Research Focus.

Now answer the following questions:

1. Is the monitoring and diagnostic assessment of reading mentioned in your school or departmental policies?

2. (a) If 'yes' is the answer, is the amount of information given sufficient for you to implement reading monitoring and diagnostic assessment appropriately?

    (b) If 'no' is the answer, why do you think this is the case?

3. Why might it be a good idea to implement these practices regardless of whether they are mentioned in policies?

Some teachers might feel it is more important to spend their time teaching their subject than worry about whether all their students have adequate reading skills. To help us understand how multifaceted the role of reading is in the secondary curriculum, read the case study below about the role of reading during one day in the life of a Year 9 class.

Case study: The role of reading during one day in the life of a Year 9 class

This is what a 'typical' Year 9 mixed class of middle-ability students was asked to do by way of reading on one fairly normal, busy school day. Their history teacher asked the students to work individually and read a range of short texts. They then had to distil the most important facts into a synopsis of an event or a period in history. The science teacher asked the students to work in pairs and read, understand and follow a set of instructions, with each partner in the pair checking the other to make sure they were both following the instructions. In English the students worked in small groups, reading and responding to a poem by creating a short dramatic sequence illustrating an interpretation of their own. In art, a short poem was projected throughout the whole lesson onto one of the studio walls, accompanied by some dreamy music. The students were asked to sketch a landscape study that they felt matched the poem and the music. In other words, each subject teacher used reading as a tool for learning in quite different ways.

Discussion

This case study makes us think about reading from the students' perspective. We realise that reading has a very instrumental aspect to it that goes far beyond checking whether vocabulary is understood, or whether the student can read aloud fluently. Those two skills are important, but we need to keep our eye on the applications to which we put reading just as much as the basic and higher-order skills of reading.

Activity 6.2   What we know about monitoring and diagnostic assessment

1. Retrieve any relevant information you gathered on monitoring and diagnostic assessment during your initial training. This will probably be in the form of guidance specific to your subject. If you have nothing from your initial training to work from, you can still get some good starting-point ideas by spending a few minutes reflecting on how you have been monitoring student progress in your subject.

2. Try filling in column 1 in Table 6.1 below with ideas drawn from your subject.

3. Now try filling in column 2 by amending the purposes to the context of reading improvement.

Table 6.1   Ideas for monitoring student learning

What I do to monitor student learning in my subject	How my approach might be adapted for monitoring reading improvement

4. Compare your ideas for columns 1 and 2 with those in the following case study on monitoring and diagnostic assessment of reading.

A valuable starting point for introducing monitoring and diagnostic assessment of reading is to look at good practice in the primary school and build from there. Chapter 2 in this book shows the value of taking the best from primary practice for improving the reading curriculum, and here the same point applies in relation to monitoring and assessment. An advantage of this approach, as is shown in the following case study, is that the approach can be kept on a small scale, and not develop into a massive and expensive school-wide commitment involving every child.

Case study: Small-scale reading monitoring and diagnostic assessment in Year 7

Jim has 10 years' teaching experience. He is Director of English and Communication in a large new eight-form-entry suburban academy for 11–16-year-olds. The academy has resulted from the amalgamation of two secondary schools. Jim knew that Key Stage 4 reading test results varied widely across the feeder primary schools, some being very poor. This concerned him, so he visited the one primary school whose results were consistently strongest over time in order to find out more.

Jim found that the primary school used a whole-school approach to target and strengthen students with weak reading skills in Years 5 and 6. A series of four-week interventions to tackle decoding and comprehension problems was then provided. These were led by two teaching assistants who had received a short specialist training course in reading problem interventions. The key to the scheme's success, Jim was told, was that each student's performance was monitored before and after each inter-vention, and that these assessments helped to diagnose whether the intervention had worked, and where further support was needed.

Jim planned a similar approach for his school, starting with Year 7. He put his proposal to the senior management team (SMT) who approved his plan and gave him and his Key Stage 3 English co-ordinator one extra lesson each of non-contact time and the use of two curriculum support assistants (CSAs) for three lessons a week each.

Jim identified the critical 10 per cent of each year group with decoding problems by running a commercially available single-word recognition test. The staff also identified the lowest-performing 10 per cent of students for whom reading compre-hension was a major challenge. Here they used the York Assessment of Reading Comprehension test (also commercially available). Jim was quite surprised to find that although each test identified 24 low reading ability students, not all students needed support for both decoding *and* comprehension. His Key Stage 3 co-ordinator worked out a carousel of sessions and groups. Together they planned a series of teaching programmes for the CSAs to deliver as interventions. Each programme was to run for four weeks on a once-a-week basis. Homework and a special 20 minutes a week per student of mentoring time were also included in the programmes.

After two terms, during which a total of three decoding and two comprehension programmes had run, Jim was able to report considerable progress to his SMT. The initial screening tests had revealed a total of 32 students in need of help. Of these, 20 received all five programmes, eight students received only the decoding programmes and four received comprehension support only. All 32 students' reading scores had improved considerably. Furthermore, improvements in attitude were clear in all the students: they were far more positive towards school and learning, and the overall verdict of their subject teachers (stated in a quick survey) was that they were very impressed by the impact of the reading interventions on improving the students' progress across the curriculum.

Discussion

The key to Jim's success was that he applied sound but very basic assessment principles. First, he researched the problem by looking for and examining a successful model; second, he adapted the model to suit his own school's circumstances; third, SMT approval and resources gave his plans a good measure of authority; fourth, he kept his interventions to a manageable scale; fifth, he targeted the interventions to students' needs; and, finally, he made sure he had clear 'before' and 'after' data.

Possible deficits in Key Stages 3 and 4 students' learning and how these might be addressed

It is important to understand why some older students have not acquired good reading habits. Without some knowledge of the causes of reading problems our attempts to remedy them may misfire. You may by now have come to appreciate that broadly speaking there are three major groups of problems exhibited by students with reading problems: a lack of adequate decoding skills; poor reading comprehension skills; or both. Researchers have found that establishing the nature of the reading problem is an essential first step in improving a student's reading (see the Simple View of Reading in Chapter 1).

Research focus: Types of reading deficits among older students

The following paragraph is summarised from a 2011 online report of some UK research that shows us the potential scale of reading deficits. To read the research report in full, see: www.yarcsupport.co.uk/documents/DrSueStothard_ReadingdifficultiesatSecondaryLevel_June2011.pdf

In the report, the researchers warned that secondary students may have reading difficulties that are going unnoticed. This study of 857 students in 28 state schools in England by researchers at the University of York found that around one in seven had reading ages of two years or more below their actual age. The study also found that 53 per cent of children with significant reading problems were on the special educational needs (SEN) register. But a 15-year-old student who had a reading age of just eight years and nine months was not on the register. The researchers added that, as some children may be on the SEN register for difficulties other than reading problems, the findings could be an underestimate.

Many teachers are aware that dyslexia is a commonly used term that may cover a wide range of reading and language problems. For example, one of the UK's leading researchers on dyslexia has identified the following as typical markers of dyslexia:

$\longrightarrow$

- poor reading fluency;

- slow speed of writing;

- poor organisation and expression in work;

- difficulties in phonological awareness, verbal memory and verbal processing speed.

(adapted from Bonifacci and Snowling, 2008)

You can see from this that there are several possible types of reading problem among secondary older students. It is quite possible that a student who has not been diagnosed as dyslexic, or who has been assessed as not having dyslexia, may nevertheless exhibit one or more of the traits on Bonifacci and Snowling's list. In addition to the traits on that list, accounts of reading problems among older students often suggest additional signs of sources of problems, such as letter and word recognition, understanding words and ideas and general vocabulary skills. This gives the subject teacher quite a range of difficulties to consider.

Some intervention programmes and resources

An excellent guide to a wide range of resources for primary and secondary schools to use with students experiencing reading difficulties has been produced by Greg Brooks (2013) (*What works for children and young people with literacy difficulties?*, downloadable at: www.interventionsforliteracy.org.uk). This is a scholarly yet highly readable publication giving information about the effectiveness of a number of reading resources. In Chapter 3, Part B, p. 21, Brooks sets out in Table 3.3 all the resources for Years 7, 8 and 9 that he has sifted through and evaluated.

Two examples of schemes that Brooks evaluates are *Corrective Reading* (McGraw-Hill) and *Sound Training for Reading*. *Corrective Reading* targets students who are reading at one or more years below their chronological age. It covers decoding and comprehension and provides a set of workbooks. It runs on an intensive system on a short-term basis, delivered by teachers and TAs. Usefully, bearing in mind points made earlier in Chapter 5 about the need for reading skills to allow students to apply and use information from texts, the Comprehension strand includes 'Concept Applications'. Brooks cites one school that found that a programme of six lessons a fortnight showed substantial improvement in reading.

Sound Training for Reading was designed to help students in Key Stage 3 with reading difficulties, although it is now used in Key Stage 2 and Key Stage 4 as well. Students in groups of four attend six one-hour sessions over a period of six weeks. The delivery is very intensive and very repetitive, using multisensory teaching methods. The students are explicitly taught syllabification. As the name suggests, there is heavy concentration on sounds of vowels and consonants. An interesting and perhaps unusual feature of this scheme is that it also contains a set of lessons devoted to speed reading. Fluency in reading is often underappreciated as a skill that students should acquire. However, it is very important that readers maintain good pace and flow in their reading because unduly slow reading can impede their comprehension. Slow reading pace can cause an increased load on cognitive processes. The reader loses understanding as information fades from working memory.

Evaluation evidence for *Sound Training for Reading* is limited, as it was carried out on an experimental group by the author of the scheme in one school. However, while the experimental group of students made a modest gain in reading, the comparison group fell steadily further behind, so that the experimental group's gain might be seen as considerably greater than the comparison group's.

Examples of subject heads running assessments and interventions

Even though we have to treat evidence with care, ideas that seem to work are always worth considering. If you are a subject head of department or faculty who is thinking about introducing some kind of literacy or reading policy, it might help to read some mini case studies of subject departments in different schools that have introduced just that. Please note, these are cases of reading assessments and interventions that have been developed at departmental rather than whole-school level. Here are four examples that illustrate how such departments have adapted existing ideas for their own purposes.

> ### Case studies: Four examples of departments that run successful reading policies
>
> 1. Michaela is director of modern foreign languages (MFLs) in an urban academy. She has long been aware that, as many entrants into Year 7 have not reached Level 4, or at least are not secure enough in their Level 4s to be making swift progress towards Level 5 reading, the introduction of an MFL is for some quite a challenge. Michaela felt sure that some simple interventions, or classroom procedures, might be brought in and made standard for the lower sets. These would be aimed at simplifying the steps the students needed to take and making the MFL more accessible. Her first step was to introduce laminated cards of new vocabulary groups based on topics covered in the learning programmes. The MFL words were on one side of these cards and were colour-coded for nouns, verbs, adjectives and adverbs. Nouns and adjectives were coded red and pink respectively; verbs and adverbs were coded deep yellow and black. Michaela's only concern in colour-coding was her knowledge that there would be a small proportion of students for whom distinguishing between certain colours was difficult. She took advice from SEN staff and avoided blue, green and brown. This limited the scale of the potential

⟶

colour-discrimination problem. On the back of the cards was written the English equivalent of each word. In addition, Michaela asked the A level art group to produce some small cartoons on separate cards to help identify pairs of nouns and adjectives. The cards were a great success with all. They made vocabulary learning more fun as well as helping to embed the students' understanding of the differences between word classes, and what went with what.

These cards were only the start. Michaela asked each Year 7 to Year 9 MFL teacher to create two new language-based puzzles or games. These were shared across the full department. She was amazed to find her colleagues had between them a stock of 22 puzzles and games, all of which could be simplified for lower-set Year 7s.

Once the focus on aiding these students with their reading became shared across the department, those MFL staff who actually taught the lower Year 7 sets became more confident and competent themselves in supporting their students' reading. They created links with their sets' English staff, who introduced similar cards, puzzles and games to consolidate their students' language awareness.

2. Richard is head of science in a small rural comprehensive in north-eastern England. He felt that his students' reading was being held back by their low understanding of how reading is a skill to use across the curriculum. As preparation towards Key Stage 4, he introduced into all Year 9 science groups a short, four-week intensive intervention on language in science. He ran the intervention programme during the summer term. It took the form of 12 lessons in which he carefully planned group-based 'curiosity kits' similar to those he had heard about for reading in the primary school. Each 'curiosity kit' comprised a strong drawstring bag containing up to three items. These items were clues – either written or consisting of one object and two written clues. The task was to find out the identity of the topic for each bag. For example, the topic 'an oak tree' was represented in one bag by an acorn, a short poem by Johnny Ray Ryder with the words 'oak tree' removed, and a small piece of wood (supposedly oak!). Here's the poem Richard used, without any deletions.

The Oak Tree

A mighty wind blew night and day
It stole the oak tree's leaves away
Then snapped its boughs and pulled its bark
Until the oak was tired and stark

But still the oak tree held its ground
While other trees fell all around
The weary wind gave up and spoke.
How can you still be standing Oak?

The oak tree said, I know that you
Can break each branch of mine in two

Carry every leaf away
Shake my limbs, and make me sway
But I have roots stretched in the earth
Growing stronger since my birth
You'll never touch them, for you see
They are the deepest part of me

Until today, I wasn't sure
Of just how much I could endure
But now I've found, with thanks to you
I'm stronger than I ever knew

(Johnny Ray Ryder, retrieved 15 January 2014 from: http://lessonsoftheoaktree. blogspot.co.uk/2009/02/we-are-all-children.html)

Richard found he was quite inventive with these 'curiosity kits', and made some of them really hard to work out. The students loved them.

3. Sam, a computer programming and technology teacher, could see that reading was not a very gripping aspect of his subject. Students' expectations seemed to be that reading was of low consequence in his field so they didn't need to bother in his lessons. He also realised that they had picked up this message from him! In his eagerness to engage their interest, he had simplified his lesson materials so much that he had virtually removed the written word altogether. Reading was absent from his lessons. Sam decided to create short reading-based tasks as an introduction to each lesson. These were devised as group exercises, and required each group to read and follow a short set of instructions. These were usually in the form of a piece of information about the topic and a small number of tasks that got the group ready for the main input of the lesson. Sam also introduced the practice of groups reading to other groups their summary reports of each week's lessons and voting for the best one. Each member of the group that produced the best-read (not written, although the groups did their best to produce good writing) report of the week gained a house point.

4. Lee, a secondary music teacher, felt that the concept of music notation was so alien to one of his classes that he introduced a regular challenge or competition – notation reading and word reading. This took the form of a quiz every four weeks that consisted of questions in which a few notes of music on a simple stave had to be translated into letters. These were mixed in with music knowledge questions. The quiz was printed and students had to read the questions and then write down their answers. Each time, Lee gave out small prizes for the winner and the most improved student.

Discussion

These departmental interventions show how simple it can be to introduce a little emphasis upon reading in a helpful and enjoyable way. It's almost as if students need to be helped to remember that reading is not only something you do in

English, but is a cross-curricular skill that they need to call upon all the time. Michaela's use of laminated cards with word classes differentiated by colour to introduce new vocabulary may well have reminded her students of similar approaches in their primary schools. The point is that Michaela's use of various word puzzles and games engaged the MFL students' attention through the medium of reading. Richard's 'curiosity kits' succeeded in focussing his students' learning through investigating links between textual features and objects. The reading was at the same time vital and incidental. Sam's requirement of reading text aloud as part of each week's group reports raised the profile both of reading and writing. Lee's quizzes helped students use reading in a regular, enjoyable way.

Some strategies for working with colleagues to develop a whole-school approach across curricular areas

As teachers committed to improving students' reading so that they can access all learning experiences across the curriculum, it sounds really attractive to have a whole school literacy policy in place and operating effectively. An ideal state for a whole-school literacy policy in place and operating effectively. An ideal state for a secondary school, one might say. However, it isn't an easy goal to achieve and you need a number of necessary conditions to be in place. Research has a lot to tell us about introducing whole-school policies.

Research focus: Introducing whole-school policies in secondary schools

Much of the apparent research evidence about introducing whole-school reading policies is in the form of self-reports from case studies of schools that have gone through this process. By Googling the term 'Whole School Reading Policies' you will find a great many of these. They are very interesting and stimulating to read, perhaps even encouraging. We do have to be a little cautious about accepting these, however, because by nature these reports are from successful schools that are naturally very keen to present their experiences to the world. What we don't find so many examples of, however, are cases that have failed, or not worked out as planned. So the recommended reading at the end of this chapter lists some helpful advice sheets and guides from national bodies and institutions that have gathered and sifted evidence from many cases of schools, some successful and others less so, before arriving at their recommendations. The advice contained within these guides is more reliable because their content has been reviewed objectively and weighed against potential counter-evidence before being made public.

⟶

Much research recommends the following three main steps for secondary schools to consider.

1. Sufficient data already exists that can reasonably screen all students entering secondary schools and identify those needing some form of reading support. Secondary schools should include for consideration any evidence from other subject areas, such as mathematics. In other words, for secondary schools to run their own screening tests in order to identify at-risk readers is a costly and somewhat inefficient use of their resources.

2. Given that SATs and primary school advice are likely to be sufficient sources of screening evidence, the most effective next step for secondary schools is to focus the intervention (support) they offer into two forms – comprehension support and decoding support. More students are likely to be in need of the former, although some will need both and some will need decoding as an initial and very essential basic building block. Teaching comprehension skills is a specialist activity, requiring the tutor (who may be a teacher, classroom assistant, learning support assistant, etc.) to work on the transition from decoding to understanding meaning, and then on to applying and using that knowledge. The student's cognitive processes need to be developed.

3. Concentrated, intensive bursts of teaching reading skills (whether decoding, comprehension or a mix) are more likely to be successful than more drip-feed approaches run over several weeks or terms. So it will be more effective for a group of Year 7 (for example) students who entered secondary school with low Level 3 reading to be taught in three 50-minute sessions each week for four weeks than one 50-minute session for 12 weeks. There has to be a drive and impetus to the reading support that cannot exist on a once-a-week basis. The support programme is more effective if it is not replacing an English lesson.

It is worth remembering that there will be some students for whom reading may never become a fluent and straightforward process, however well they are supported. Also, for some older students, their reading problem is the consequence of an unsatisfactory or disrupted experience of learning to read at the primary school. Of course, this may have been caused by a wide range of possible factors, or mixture of factors, many psychological or social in origin.

There are two key messages arising from the objective evidence about introducing whole-school reading policies. The first is to start small scale and grow organically, increasing on a planned basis to whole-school scale. The second is to make the change for the whole school in one step. The gradual approach is far more likely to make the policy become fully embedded than would result from introducing wholesale change.

The second key message is to bring influential others with you. This usually means school leaders, the higher up the school system the better. Also, don't forget that governors and parents need to be on board.

Case study: Introducing and leading a whole-school approach to literacy across the secondary curriculum

A secondary school in north Yorkshire has established a strong literacy curriculum across all subjects, and within all lessons. Training has been delivered in dedicated CPD slots across the year; and one of the teaching and learning coaching team has been selected to work in the primary feeder school as well as the secondary school to aid transition and share good practice. This has had an impact on the literacy of both schools. The primary school has gained insight into the teaching methods of a secondary school and the secondary school has learned that carrying on the good literacy practices of the primary school phase is essential to the progress of its students. Key to this is phonics, and now all teachers have received training and regularly deliver games, starters and whole lessons where spelling, phonics and reading have a much higher profile than before.

However, maintaining this and tracking its success has become crucial if this approach is to become embedded. The school has put several measures in place to ensure continuation, training and enthusiasm.

- Each department has *a literacy co-ordinator* who is responsible for the implementation of new initiatives, ideas and training.

- Each classroom has to display phonics in the word banks and on learning walls. Key words and spellings are highlighted, breaking words down into syllables, word webs and affixes where appropriate.

- Termly innovative practice is discussed and shared across faculties in designated CPD sessions where each faculty – not just English – leads a session where they share their good practice concerning delivery of literacy within their subject.

- Regular starters and ideas are emailed to staff to use instantly in their lessons and their tutor time to help keep the phonics and reading agenda high on the list of priorities.

- Senior leadership team members (SLT) and heads of faculty are involved in *literacy learning walks* around the school – as an inspirational tool rather than a checking tool – although clearly it serves as both.

- Literacy strategies from each faculty are summarised and published to parents on the website and discussed in parent forums held by the school.

- The special needs team receive additional coaching to work with vulnerable students where their understanding of basic phonics lags behind their peers.

- Icons are used as well as words on posters/ppts/tasks around the school and are common to all classrooms, e.g.: a pencil at the side of the instruction 'write . . .'

- The yearly faculty review will stress that literacy and reading will be a feature that is expected to be evident and commented on in a formal assessment.

$\longrightarrow$

The school has a senior leader overseeing this who works closely with both the primary liaison coach and the English department – this is key to keeping the profile high and relevant. Training faculties in basic phonics and then making it relevant to their lessons, their learning environments and their planning across the entire curriculum is essential if a whole-school approach is to succeed. Tracking it and seeing that it is happening through shared experiences as well as formalised assessments is important if it is to become second nature to all staff.

Discussion

The ideas in this case study, especially the bullet points about embedding the policy, are simple and straightforward. Perhaps the most costly, in terms of financial resource, is to identify a *literacy co-ordinator* for every department, because they need a small weekly allocation of non-contact time in which to perform their tasks. Other ideas are very low cost. The *learning walks for literacy* conducted by SLT can also have other purposes incorporated into them; for example, the very act of the SLT being seen out and about more will help staff feel supported and make students more aware of the need to focus on their learning. Another of the ideas, *extra phonics coaching for the SEN team*, might have the additional benefit of helping them feel more supported in their role too. It is worth looking through Chapter 3 of this book, the chapter on challenges, for valuable content for such sessions.

This case study also highlights the importance of tracking and monitoring. Often, *evaluation* of a whole-school policy is seen as the overriding feature, with the consequence that the follow-up to issues raised by monitoring and tracking systems is perhaps overlooked, or demoted. As tracking and monitoring policy is often a lever to raise students' attainment or performance, then quantifiable improvements in students' scores are important. Many reports of school-wide policy implementations say little about tracking and monitoring. Often schools assume that the measures they have put in place will take care of themselves. It's almost as if the evaluation outcomes of the policy override making sure that students themselves are experiencing the developments as planned.

Nearly all schools in the UK have developed their own or bought commercial information management systems (MISs). These are, essentially, databases on which many aspects of students' attainments in assessments can be recorded. These MISs provide the essential foundation stone for monitoring and tracking. Schools then set targets upon which regular reports from the databases can be produced. Tracking and monitoring are inseparable parts of the same system; in effect they are two sides of the same coin. Tracking students' progress reveals whether they are improving as readers, and at what rate of progress. Tracking is very much at the level of the individual student. Monitoring the data that the tracking system provides is a means of checking at cohort level that the intended policy changes are taking place and that the policy is being effective. With respect to addressing reading difficulties, they can help you target needy students and determine whether your support is being effective.

Learning outcomes review

You should now be aware of:

1. methods for monitoring students' progress and diagnostic assessment;
2. possible deficits in Key Stage 3 and 4 students' learning and how these might be addressed;
3. a range of intervention programmes and resources;
4. some strategies for working with colleagues to develop a whole-school approach across curricular areas.

Self-assessment questions

1. What is monitoring?
2. What is the value of diagnostic assessment?
3. What is the value of a whole-school approach to reading?

Activities: answers and discussion

Activity 6.1   Thinking about why we monitor and assess progress

1.   Yes, but only in passing.

2.   (a) Not enough to help me get to grips with how to monitor and assess reading diagnostically. Tends to assume I as a teacher in the school know what to do.

   (b) Possibly monitoring and assessment of reading has been thought of more as a primary school concern. Maybe it has never been pointed out by an inspection team or by a local authority learning improvement team.

3.   I suppose a good reason might be that the more I undertake monitoring and assessment of reading, the more I can see whether what I'm doing is having any effect.

Activity 6.2   What we know about monitoring and diagnostic assessment

Table 6.1   Ideas for monitoring student learning

What I do to monitor student learning in my subject	How my approach might be adapted for monitoring reading improvement
Keep a note in my class register of any student who seems to be struggling with reading	Try to identify what kind of texts cause student to struggle
Tell the SEN co-ordinator of such cases, when I remember to	Try to find out the nature of the reading problems
Try to differentiate group work by degree of reading skill required	See if SEN co-ordinator can provide any support in any way

Further reading

The National Strategies document *Practical strategies to support the whole school development of AfL with APP (Primary)* is well worth reading. Many helpful ideas in it can be used in secondary schools. It is cached at: www.core.kmi.open.ac.uk/download/pdf/4150821.pdf

A very readable and well informed short paper on introducing inclusive practices at a whole school level can be found at www.tlrp.org/pub/documents/no6_ainscow.pdf. Again, the focus is not quite on reading, but the advice is very clear and accessible. Everything it offers is well supported by research evidence.

The Guardian Teacher Network has a really lively and fascinating account of a project on getting the whole school reading. Look at: www.theguardian.com/teacher-network/2011/nov/28/whole-school-reading to read a report of the November 2011 workshop on 'The Magic of Whole School Reading'. The subtitle is 'How to turn your school into a "reading school"! Drop everything and read!' You may wish to sign up to the network too.

Finally, best of all is probably the advice from two items on the National Literacy Trust website. One is about developing a whole-school reading policy, which you can find at: www.literacytrust.org.uk/assets/0000/7721/Developing_your_whole-school_reading_culture.pdf. This really does take a step-by-step approach that takes full account of how the realities of school life need to be managed in achieving this goal. It includes a link to a reading audit that includes Key Stage 4, and guidance about the kind of timeline you might work to, with sensible objectives en route.

The second item is aimed directly at secondary schools and is more of a guide to how literacy awareness can be raised among teachers and effectively taught by them in secondary schools. This can be found at: www.literacytrust.org.uk/assets/0001/4462/The_Literacy_Guide_for_Secondary_Schools_2012-13__EXTRACT.pdf

References

Bonifacci, P. & Snowling, M. J. (2008) Speed of processing and reading disability: A cross-linguistic investigation of dyslexia and borderline intellectual functioning. *Cognition,* 107 (3): 999–1017doi: 10.1016/j.cognition.2007.12.006

Brooks, G. (2013) What works for children and young people with literacy difficulties? 4th edition (downloadable at: www.interventionsforliteracy.org.uk).

Fuchs, L. S. and Fuchs, D. (1999) Monitoring student progress toward the development of reading competence: A review of three forms of classroom-based assessment. *School Psychology Review*, 28 (4): 659–71.

Safer, N. and Fleischman, S. (2005) How schools improve. *Educational Leadership*, 62 (5): 81–3.

Index